Praise for
CHASING SILHOUETTES

Chasing Silhouettes is a must-have field manual for parents, spouses and friends of disordered eaters, as well as professionals seeking greater understanding of the family aspects of this struggle. Written in the blood, sweat and tears of the author and her family, and featuring expert clinical perspectives, *Chasing Silhouettes* blazes a trail of hope and practical insight for all who long to help but don't know how.

Constance Rhodes
Founder and CEO, FINDINGbalance, Inc.

As a pastor, teacher and director of a ministry that works directly with young women who are in the healing process dealing with anorexia nervosa, I know how critically vital and helpful the information in this book is. Perhaps most importantly, I know this on a very personal level. As the mother of a daughter who struggled for 10 long years to overcome her battle with anorexia and bulimia, I sought for a 'voice' that would speak to the fears in my heart and answer my questions. I have since discovered that I was not alone, and there were more than I could have imagined who are struggling just as I did. This wonderful book will be an answer to their cry for help.

Helen Burns
Director, Mercy Ministries Canada

Where only a few authors have dared to step, Wierenga has waded in. Rather than dancing around the issues of faith and family, this work specifically addresses both faith and family as integral parts of the story—both the disorder itself, and the journey to freedom from it. Through this work, Wierenga is doing a great service to the millions of Americans affected by anorexia nervosa. She is speaking truth into a community that is lost, and far too often hopeless.

Carylynn Larson, Ph.D.
Director, Rock Recovery

I have been waiting a long time for a book that speaks directly to the loved ones of persons struggling with eating disorders. Well researched with professional input, Emily Wierenga provides a comprehensive resource that addresses the whole person: physically, emotionally, mentally, relationally and spiritually. With thoughtfulness and insight, she tenderly points the way to hope and healing in Christ.

Ann Capper, RD, CDN
Nutrition Editor, FINDINGbalance, Inc.

This book depicts an honest view of the powerful impact of an eating disorder, not just on the person struggling but on everyone involved. As the former assistant clinical director at Remuda Ranch Treatment Center for Eating Disorders, I am highly impressed with Emily Wierenga's ability to weave together her story within a therapeutically sound framework, integrating the context for recovery from a Christian perspective. This is a book worth reading to gain insight into the healing process from an eating disorder.

Amy E. Wasserbauer, Ph.D.
Clinical Psychologist,
Renewed Hope Counseling and Psychological Services

With this sinister disease, it is imperative the individual address recovery on three fronts: mind, body and soul. I highly recommend *Chasing Silhouettes* to those who want to ensure they are addressing the spiritual side of their recovery. It offers insight and guidance for the victim and family not found in other approaches.

Ron Broughton, M.Ed., L.P.C.
Chief Clinical Officer, Brookhaven Hospital

In *Chasing Silhouettes*, you will find truth, honesty, and vulnerability. You will find hope, healing, and encouragement. It is an intimate discussion with people who have been there themselves. The reader who picks up this book feeling hopeless and ill-equipped to overcome an eating disorder will find its pages brimming with light.

Christie Pettit
Author, Empty: A Story of Anorexia *(Revell, 2006)*

Many in recovery from an eating disorder do not have the denial of facts, but have the denial of impact on their loved ones. Too often these heartaches are not validated. Less often are they lovingly guided. As the director of family services for an inpatient eating disorder facility, I am always looking for resources to recommend to families that hurt alongside their loved ones. I believe *Chasing Silhouettes* is an important and necessary resource for families in need.

Todd R. Davis, M.A. LMHC
Family Therapist, Selah House

Chasing Silhouettes may well be one of the most important books published for the church this year. That's right, I said for the church. Because eating disorders don't just happen outside the church; they happen in the church, too, to pastors' daughters like Wierenga. And the church can do great good – and great harm – in how it responds. The book is a painful read. It is also a hopeful read.

Glynn Young
The High Calling

Emily's writing (has) helped me to heal more than my days in an eating disorder unit. Although they offered some good habits and a few ideas on how I got to where I was, my soul never found healing in that place. Emily's writings offer healing to my soul and I want to pass that on to other families.

- Anonymous Reader

After 20 years with an eating disorder, I'm finally seeing the light.

- Anonymous Reader

chasing silhouettes

HOW TO HELP A LOVED ONE BATTLING AN EATING DISORDER

EMILY T. WIERENGA

Requests for information should be addressed to:
Ampelon Publishing
PO Box 140675
Boise, ID 83714

Published in association with MacGregor Literary, Hillsboro, Oregon.

To order other Ampelon Publishing products, visit us on the web at:
www.ampelonpublishing.com

Cover design: Morgan Wolf
Cover photo: © iStockphoto/airportrait

Printed on paper and with ink made from sustainable resources

To my family:
Without your love, I would no longer be alive

Table of Contents

FOREWORD

by Gregory L. Jantz, Ph.D.

AS A SPECIALIST IN the field of eating disorders for more than 30 years, I know well the role that relationships play in the complexities of the disease. Be it anorexia, bulimia, binge eating, or compulsive eating, how we communicate with one another can mean the difference between hope and hopelessness.

Unfortunately, we cannot rely on years of knowing and loving one another to inform this process, as there is a stranger in our midst. For someone living with an eating disorder, every conversation is heard through the filter of the disease—a disorder of the mind that skews and colors the truth of every situation and relationship. So what are we to do?

Certainly, educating ourselves with expert advice from medical professionals is key. But equally important is seeking out testimony from those in recovery, and the family and friends who are, for all intents and purposes, in recovery with them.

Of course, whether we know it or not, embedded at the core of every relationship in our lives is the most important of all—our relationship with God. Yet eating disorders, by their very nature, aim to cut that spiritual tie. Among other things, our Creator intends us to seek out nourishment and strength for our bodies, a form of self-love necessary to sustain ourselves for the loving and caring of others. Starving ourselves as a plea for help (i.e., love), or overeating as a means of filling a seemingly loveless void, distract us from the only thing that can *truly* sustain us—daily feeding of our spiritual selves.

Yet considering the all-important, key role played by relationships—with God and with one another—in the healing process, both are historically absent from eating disorder treatment programs. It is for this reason that I developed the "whole-person" approach to treatment utilized for all of my faith-based recovery programs at The Center for Counseling and Health Resources in Edmonds, Washington. This whole-person approach naturally incorporates attention to the physical, intellectual, and emotional side of things, but also to the relational and spiritual that are all-too-often neglected, with the most tragic of consequences.

It is rare I find a resource that so uniquely supplements the whole-person approach to eating disorder treatment as what I have discovered in this insightful, inspiring book.

In addition to the perspective of health professionals, what's at the heart of *Chasing Silhouettes* is Emily's story as told through her relationships. And what this story brings to the world of eating disorder treatment is not only a voice for those living with the disease, but a voice for the family and friends desperate to help.

Whatever your own personal experience with the disease, you will see some of yourself in the pages of this book. Are you a parent filled with guilt? Are you a sibling filled with resentment? Are you a friend filled with confusion? Are you a spouse filled with despair? Are you a child filled with fear? Or are you the one *living* with the eating disorder, filled with *all* of these feelings but devoid of what you need to feel most—love?

Throughout this book, Emily, her family, and her friends bravely and poignantly share their sobering testimonies from the most desperate of perspectives. But eloquently weaved into every page is the thread of hope they all held onto in helping Emily find her way to recovery. That's not to say they felt themselves on the road to success anywhere along the way. In fact, what Emily and her loved ones express most are their thoughts and feelings of uncertainty, at a loss of what to say or do.

Thankfully, though, they were never at a loss of what to *pray*. Emily's parents and siblings speak at length about the role prayer has played in helping them navigate their way through this disease. And Emily includes a number of inspiring prayers throughout the book, as well as frequent insights into how her recovery has hinged upon her faith.

In the whole-person approach to eating disorder treatment and recovery, I highly recommend this whole-*family* perspective that

Emily Wierenga has so generously shared here. This is a whole-family that includes parents, siblings, spouses, children, and friends, as well as the most unconditionally loving family member of all: our Father.

"For I know the plans I have for you," declares the Lord, "plans to prosper you and not to harm you, plans to give you hope and a future." ~Jeremiah 29:11

Gregory L. Jantz, Ph.D.
Founder of The Center for Counseling and Health Resources
Author of *Hope, Help & Healing for Eating Disorders:
A New Approach to Treating Anorexia, Bulimia, and Overeating*
(Shaw, 2002)

PROLOGUE

DEAR EXHAUSTED READER,

I was that girl you are trying to save. The one who is all rib and screaming and slamming of door, the one who once laughed, who now wants to die. And this is killing you.

And I wish I could hug you now and say, while I *was* that girl, I'm now a woman who wants desperately to live.

I was 13 and purple with hypothermia, "a miracle," the doctors said, but all I could see was the mistake God had made in making me.

And it was four years of not eating. Four years of insulting the mother who homeschooled me, the pastor-father who worked day and night to put bread and granola on the table and it wasn't enough, I told them.

And I wish I could hug you and tell you that it is enough. *You are enough*, and one day, you'll laugh with your loved one again. One day you'll sit across the table from her and share a meal with her, for we serve a God who rocks at redemption.

A God who celebrates the losers, but who often waits until we're forced to give up and then—only then—does He step in.

I can't explain why I decided to eat again, except for the way I saw myself clearly one day for the skeleton I was. And I wanted then, more than anything, to be normal. To go to school and to crush on boys and to write papers and go to slumber parties and to stop counting calories.

It was never about the food, and all about the scapegoats. Eventually, we're left emptier for trying to pass the blame.

And in the end, it's love we're starving for.

It's easy to not want our loved ones to feel something for the pain it causes them. But we need to let them cry, and to hold them when they do. To not fix.

Then they'll know their sadness means something, that they are worth the feeling.

And this girl, the one who's writing you, she's now desperately happy.

So rest, friend. Rest and get your strength back and trust and hope, for a new day is dawning.

In Him,
e.

INTRODUCTION

SHE WOULD TELL ME God loved me. She would say I was beautifully and wonderfully made, because God had made me that way, and the Bible tells me so, and I wanted to believe her with all of my eight-year-old heart, but I couldn't.

Maybe it was moving so often or not being able to choose what I wore or watched or played with or read, or maybe it was how Mum looked longingly at her flower beds, twisting apron in hand, as I stood, a clumsy daughter, before her.

Whatever it was, I didn't care what God thought. I only cared about what Mum thought. Whether *she* thought I was beautiful.

Soon, I didn't even care about that anymore.

***

It's hard to parent in today's world. This place of MTV and super-models. This place where appearance is seemingly everything, and society tells us *body image* is what people see, not the intrinsic value of the skin we wear. This place in which 80 percent of young people are dieting, and being fat is more feared, surveys say, than nuclear war, cancer or losing one's parents.

This book is not a manual. It's not a self-help resource. I wish I could offer you 10 steps towards fixing your loved one's broken body image, but I cannot. I can, however, direct you to the One who is more than able.

Chasing Silhouettes is intended to be a spiritual guide to help families redefine body image, as well as to offer insight for caregivers into the minds and hearts of those battling an eating disorder.

As someone who battled anorexia nervosa, both as a child and as an adult, I am here to offer you hope. Our young people, our loved ones, do not have to be defeated by the lies that permeate culture today. But in order to defeat these lies, we need to understand the truth.

Throughout the pages of this book, I will share my story, and shine a light on the thoughts—complicated as they are—which your loved one is probably experiencing. I will unveil the lessons my parents and siblings learned as they helped me to recover the first time at the age of 13, and I will talk with faith-based professionals who work in the field of eating disorders. And then, I will pray with you, and help you to wait on God as your loved one struggles.

We cannot fix our children. But He can.

Defining Eating Disorders

According to the National Eating Disorder Association, 10 million females and one million males are fighting a life and death battle with an eating disorder such as anorexia or bulimia, while millions more struggle with binge eating disorder. And the effect of this on children? *Time* magazine says 80 percent have been on a diet by the time they've reached fourth grade.

As a child I made forts. I would pile couch pieces and sit beneath them and while away the world for I was queen of my cushions, my plaid thrift-store sofa fortress.

An eating disorder (ED) is a type of fortress. It's a way for a child or teenager, who feels as though the world is a scary place, to regain a sense of control, a sense of belonging.

At the same time, it's a way for children to punish themselves for whatever they did to bring on this scary side of the world. By isolating themselves, they feel as though they cannot be hurt, nor can they hurt anyone. There is comfort in this self-erected world, for it is predictable. Soon, it becomes home.

The only way to truly reach a child in his sofa fortress is to get down on all fours and knock on the cushion door and hope he or she allows you to enter.

And by sitting there, in that darkened space beneath that plaid fabric, by sharing in that comfort zone, you'll begin to understand why your child needs this space. And your child, in turn, will realize there's at least one person in the world (you) whom he or she can trust. Because you're not threatening to take away the only safe place your son or daughter knows.

If your child becomes very sick, there is no doubt you need to knock down those cushions. But otherwise, it's a waiting game. Waiting for your loved one to learn to trust, to believe, and to desire more than this cushion-shelter.

These forts take on different shapes. I'll label them for you, now.

Anorexia Nervosa

Often found in perfectionist personalities, anorexia nervosa is the refusal to eat, in an attempt to control a variety of conflicts including stress, anxiety, unhappiness, and in some cases, abuse. Recent research suggests that genetic predisposition sometimes plays a role in a person's sensitivity towards anorexia, while environmental factors serve as the trigger.

Though low self-esteem and poor body image play a role in the conception of the disease, as it develops, it turns into an obsession with control, fuelled largely by a fear of being fat.

By controlling what they eat, those with anorexia feel they can control their emotions. Some believe they do not deserve to be happy, and therefore deprive themselves of situations offering pleasure—including eating.

Signs that your child might have anorexia include obsessive exercise, calorie and fat gram counting, starvation and restriction of food, the use of diet pills, laxatives or diuretics to attempt controlling weight, and a persistent concern with body image.

Bulimia Nervosa

Those with bulimia tend to be easy-going personalities who people-please. They have a secret obsession with binging and purging. The food serves as a narcotic, by which to deal with daily stresses and unnecessary blame, and the purging relieves them of the guilt of overeating.

While triggered by low self-esteem and a desire to be in control of one's emotions, as with anorexia, bulimia is the over-indulgence of food followed by the immediate release of it all. Laxatives or self-induced vomiting help to release feelings of anger, depression, stress or anxiety. Again, genetic predisposition may play a part, with environmental factors serving as the trigger.

Signs that your loved one might have bulimia include recurring episodes of rapid food consumption followed by tremendous guilt and purging (laxatives or self-induced vomiting), a feeling of lacking control over his or her eating behaviors, regularly engaging in stringent diet plans and exercise, the misuse of laxatives, diuretics, and/or diet pills, and a persistent concern with body image. All of these are warning signs that someone is suffering from bulimia.

Binge Eating Disorder

Those who binge eat bear similar characteristics to those who eat compulsively or have bulimia. The binge eater periodically undergoes large feasts, consuming an abnormally high quantity of food in a short time period of time (under two hours), absorbing uncontrollably until uncomfortably full.

Unlike bulimia, the binging is not followed by purging. The weight of binge eaters is often above average to overweight. Sufferers tend to struggle with losing and maintaining their weight.

Reasons for overeating parallel those of compulsive overeaters; binges provide an outlet for emotions, a way to fill the emptiness, a means for coping with daily stresses and problems. Binging is a way of keeping people away, of rebelling against society by trying to not be attractive or what they see as lovable. Sufferers may feel undeserving of love, and use binging as self-punishment.

Those with Binge Eating Disorder are at risk for heart attacks, high blood pressure and cholesterol, kidney disease and/or failure, arthritis and bone deterioration, and strokes.

Compulsive Overeating

Individuals with compulsive overeating habits are "addicted" to food, using it as a way to soften life's blows. Food serves as a means for dealing with stress, for filling a void, and for hiding from painful emotions. While compulsive overeaters don't tend to binge, they eat food when they're not hungry, using it for comfort.

Compulsive overeaters tend to be overweight and are aware that their eating habits are abnormal. As with binge eaters, they often use their appearance to shield them from society, particularly if they've suffered sexual abuse. They feel guilty for never measuring up, ashamed of their weight, and struggle with very low self-esteem.

Individuals suffering from compulsive overeating are at risk for heart attacks, high blood pressure and cholesterol, kidney disease and/or failure, arthritis and bone deterioration, and strokes.

Other lesser-known forms of disordered eating include:

Calorie Prisoners: fear gaining weight, they tend to label food as good or bad and battle extreme guilt if they indulge in something that's off-limits.

Secret Eaters: sneak junk food at home, in the car, or in bed late at night—wherever they won't be discovered.

Career Dieters: don't know how to eat without a menu-plan; are constantly going on diets; despite their attempts to lose weight, tend to be overweight or obese.

Purgers: obsessed with getting rid of unwanted calories, they purge by using laxatives, diuretics or by occasionally vomiting.

Food addicts: use food as a means for soothing stress, dealing with anger, or celebrating a joyous event; food is a constant preoccupation.

Orthorexia: fixated with healthy or righteous eating.

Pregorexia: into extreme dieting and exercising while pregnant to avoid gaining the 25 to 35 pounds of weight doctors usually recommend.

Anorexia Athletica: addicted to exercise.

Drunkorexia: restrict food intake in order to reserve those calories for alcohol and binge drinking.

Diabulimia: individuals with Type 1 diabetes who deliberately administer less insulin than necessary for the purpose of weight loss.

***

While the stories in this book are based exclusively on my experience with anorexia, the advice from family members and professionals applies to all eating disorders.

Each section describes a certain stage of the battle and what to look for:

Recognizing (how to recognize when your loved one has an ED);

Reacting (how to respond, in the midst of it);

Recovery (what to do when your loved one decides to recover);

Renewal (how to help your loved one walk in health and wholeness), and

Related Accounts (stories of others who've battled an eating disorder).

Through it all, I hope to help you, as readers, redefine *body image* in light of who God made us to be, so truth might rise anew in hearts and households.

Part I

RECOGNIZING

*How to know when your loved one
has an eating disorder*

Chapter 1

Child's Perspective

My Story

THE NURSES MURMURED TO each other under fluorescent lighting as I lay shivering on the metal hospital bed. Later, I would learn that they had marveled at my hypothermic sack of bones, saying, "She should be dead." I was a breach of science, a modern-day miracle.

Yet in that profound moment, all I could think was, *Why can't I lose any more weight?*

***

It started when I began to squint my eyes for the camera. I wanted to create laughter lines in a laughter-less face.

Then I began sucking in my cheeks. I liked how it made me look thinner, model-like.

I was nine years old.

The next four years were a blur. Anorexia starved my mind, but I'll always remember the darkness. Days smudged with counting calories and streaming tears. Days filled with frowns, fierce yells and fists pounding against my father's chest.

The anorexia resulted from a number of factors.

I was rootless, having moved 10 times before the age of seven. We lived everywhere, from Ontario, to Quebec, to England, to Congo and Nigeria where my parents served as missionaries, and then back to Ontario again.

This state of constant transition left me unstable. I would begin to get attached, only to be torn up and away. I had no control over where we lived, and, being homeschooled, was very lonely. Yet my feelings didn't seem to matter. And because my father was following "the call" of God, I began to resent the faith that forced us to be "homeless."

Being the eldest of four children, my parents were strictest with me. Nothing was debatable; everything, from going to bed on time to completing chores to not being allowed to watch TV was a hard, fast rule. No discussion. If an order was broken, Mum would hand me over to Dad to be punished by a spank from his hand or a wooden spoon. No follow-up; merely pain which, over time, turned into bitterness.

Church was another regulation. I was never allowed to miss a service. Faith was a task.

I didn't understand this far-away God, but wanted to please my father who was never home—who was always visiting this church person or that. I became jealous of the people he visited. And I thought by getting baptized, perhaps I'd be "in" with my Dad's crowd and he'd call on me too.

Dad loved us by doing his job so well he put ministry before family. He'd kiss us on the cheeks early in the morning and lead Bible devotions and sigh when we asked him questions on Sermon-Writing day. I hated Sermon-Writing day.

I got baptized at age eight because Dad said I should, and I wanted to please him the same way I wanted to please God. I associated God with my father—a distant, unemotional man who said he loved me yet was too busy to show it. One year later, I realized that even though I'd gotten baptized, Dad still didn't ask me how I was doing, not really, and so God still didn't care. Not really.

Food was dished onto our plates at every meal; again, I had no choice but to finish it. This inability to make my own decisions killed my independent spirit. Mum meant well. As a nutritionist, she served healthy but plentiful portions. As a result, we became healthy but plentiful children.

Meanwhile, a woman I'd become very close to, "Grandma Ermenie," passed away. And life became even more uncontrollable, and disappointment, more certain.

I craved what I didn't have: Attention. Affirmation. Choice. My mum had never been affirmed growing up and therefore battled low self-esteem. My dad found it hard to pay compliments and was often distracted or absent. While both loved me, I grew up not feeling loved. Not knowing what it meant to be beautiful, cherished, seen or heard. As a result, I wanted nothing else.

It's a scary place to be in, this place where you have no one, so you have to become bigger than life itself in order to carry yourself through the pain. A nine-year-old isn't very big. And all I wanted was to be small. Because the world told me that thin was beauty. And maybe if I was beautiful, Dad would want to spend time with me.

I didn't know about anorexia nervosa. We weren't allowed to play with Barbie dolls or take dance lessons or look at fashion magazines or talk about our bodies in any way other than holy, so I didn't know anything except that Mum changed in the closet when Dad was in the room, and they made us cover our skin neck to foot.

A kind of shame came with this not talking about bodies, and beauty became something forbidden. And I wanted it more than anything. So I stopped eating.

It was a slow-stop, one that began with saying "No," and the "No" felt good. I refused dessert. I refused the meals Mum dished up for me. I refused the jam on my bread and then the margarine and then the bread itself.

This control over food became a gateway to my inner self; the independent spirit I'd been forced to avoid. And I began to enjoy those three tiny parts of my day—breakfast, lunch and supper—in which I could prove I was an individual.

At night, I dreamt of food. Mum would find me, hunting for imaginary chocolates in my bed. I wanted her to hug me and make the fear go away, but was worried that if she did, my guard would be let down and I'd eat real chocolates. So I stopped hugging her for two years.

My legs were getting thin, and that was what mattered, but I dreamt about Mum's arms and woke up hugging myself.

I slipped from a state of not being hungry to a state of choosing to be hungry. I liked how my pants sagged, my shirt became loose, my face slim, and my eyes, big. And at some point, I became a different person, intent on being skinny no matter the cost.

Gaining Control

I began to cut down on my daily intake of food. It started with not finishing my meals, which resulted in me not being allowed any dessert.

Unable to register that her daughter had an eating disorder, my mum, born in England, surprised me with a trip to her homeland. While there, I became resigned to bed, sick with the flu. As the flush took to my cheeks and the weight dropped from my arms, legs and face, I began to think how beautiful I was when I was sick. So the flu became an excuse for not eating.

Returning home, I was more fatigued than usual. Mum took me to the doctor's to have my blood tested. The doctor suggested she put her daughter in school. I was ecstatic; finally, a chance to have friends.

But upon arriving at school, I realized with horror how thin the girls were. How large my big-boned body was, compared to theirs. Allowed to make my own lunches, I began to abuse the new-found freedom, packing less and less each day. This resulted in a very angry, tired girl returning home each afternoon.

I was happy to finally be "normal," but sad about how ugly I felt amongst such beautiful competition. To me, "thin" represented everything I wasn't—and everything I wanted to be.

The control became addicting, and I became obsessed with "tiny." My writing shrank smaller and smaller until the teachers' eyes hurt from trying to read it. Everything in life had to be orderly and regimented. My bedroom was immaculate; my outfits, scheduled weeks ahead of time; and my journal entries, full of intricate details about each day.

Personally Speaking

It was not intended to be an eating disorder. The anorexia started innocently enough, as it does for many. For me, a beauty-seeker, it began with wanting to be found adorable and lovely. Yet as the illness worsened, it turned into an attempt to control my immediate surroundings in an otherwise haphazard world.

In a culture that not only worships skinny models but celebrates fast-food chains and over-indulgence, it is easy for children to become confused—caught up in not knowing how to indulge and still remain attractive. And in a culture where family is constantly being de-fragmented, young people are finding less and less love at home, and so, looking for it in a media-saturated, bipolar world.

Certain elements played a role in my choosing to become anorexic. These included, but were not exclusive to:

- Being the eldest of four children.
- Being a perfectionist.
- Having a sensitive heart that didn't know how to process both the pain and the beauty I beheld in the world.
- Being born to a mother with low self-esteem, and a father who put ministry before family.
- Being a person who craved freedom of choice.
- Being refused this "choice" when my parents decided what I ate at mealtime.
- Feeling insecure due to being homeschooled.
- Wanting to be found attractive by new public-school friends.
- Feeling "rootless" due to having had so many different homes growing up.

This being said, I had, overall, a very loving and Christian childhood, compared to many. My sisters and brother also underwent a similar upbringing but did not struggle with anorexia nervosa.

There is no rhyme or reason to the disease, no formula or quick solution. I wish there was, so I could offer that to you. Rather, it is largely dependent on personality and personal choice. I chose to deal with these unstable elements by controlling my eating. Another might choose to cut her hair, dress gothic, lose herself in music, or do drugs.

Eating disorders are simply this: a cry for help. And it is this cry that I wish to address.

As families, you must not lose sight of the individual doing the harm. While it may seem he or she is doing this to cause you pain, there is more to the eating disorder than meets the eye. This person is hurting, and he or she secretly yearns to be understood.

So, while it is understandable that you're worrying about the physical toll this illness might have on your child, take a moment to look more closely at his or her soul. What components make up this person? How has God made him or her unique? And how, during this scary time, can you help encourage those God-given talents and gifts versus focusing on the negative?

Your child wants to be loved. He or she may not know it, but every refusal to eat is a desperate attempt to draw you close.

Chapter 2

Parents' Perspective

Yvonne's & Ernest's Story

"SHE WON'T GET OUT of the bathroom," Yvonne Dow whispered to her husband Ernest who sat in his study preparing Sunday's sermon. "She's been in there for two hours."

Ernest looked up, brow furrowed, glasses smudged. He sighed. "It's probably nothing, right? Give her time."

Yvonne shook her head, staring at the table where her nine-year-old daughter's supper sat untouched. Once again, Emily had made an excuse about not being hungry. Was she sick? Her face had seemed flushed.

The bathroom door squeaked open, and Yvonne's eldest daughter emerged in fuzzy pink pajamas making her look far younger than she acted. She glanced over at Yvonne and scowled.

"What are you looking at?" the girl with a long, thin face, spat. Yvonne didn't know how to answer.

Emily ran upstairs and slammed her bedroom door. The whole house seemed to shake.

***

"I knew about eating disorders because I studied them in university," explains Yvonne, a 53-year-old nutritionist. "I just figured no one in my family was going to get one. It was kind of a pride thing."

Yvonne had read all of the right parenting books, served her children nutritious, wholesome meals, and raised them up to know God. She didn't let them play with Barbies, watch TV or take ballet lessons. This left no room for an eating disorder to develop; that only happened to non-Christian families with severe underlying issues. Not to hers. And so, it took a while for Yvonne to realize that indeed, her quiet daughter was starving herself.

"I knew there was a problem when Emily wasn't eating enough for a normal healthy child to maintain energy levels," she says.

Emily's father, Rev. Ernest Dow, says he noticed the anorexia more when his daughter's temper began to flare up. "She was always timid, quiet and meek—but as her body stretched up without any substance to keep pace with it, it aggravated her temper. That's when we got the slamming doors and the throwing of things…"

He pauses, trying hard to conjure up feelings long shoved down. "I felt disappointed, puzzled. We were trying to do our best in raising our family, to provide what Emily needed, but she wasn't eating. And she was getting unhealthily skinny. Also, the rebellion and rage left me at my wit's end, as Dr. Dobson's best advice didn't seem to help. It was scary because we realized (after reading some of what few books on the subject were available in the 1980s) it could be fatal."

When asked what she thinks caused the anorexia, Yvonne recalls having read that trauma often triggers an eating disorder. "The only thing I can think of is when Grandma Ermenie died. She and Emily had become quite close."

In addition to the trauma, Yvonne admits to having been a controller. Yvonne realizes now, her daughter needed choice, and regrets trying to fit Emily into a certain "mold."

Ernest says passive pride on his part also played a big role in Emily's downfall. "There was pressure for my children to be raised a certain way because they were pastor's kids—and we believed that because we home-schooled our children, they would turn out differently from the others."

Weighing in the Factors

No parent is to blame for his/her child's eating disorder. I cannot stress this enough. Children have freedom of choice, and it was by choosing to diet that your child opened him/herself up to the temptation of disordered eating.

It is important that you, as a parent, believe this, so you might be able to help your loved one. If you do not believe this and continue to blame and berate yourself, you will, ironically, only contribute to the factors that instigated your child's eating disorder in the first place.

A child derives his or her sense of worth largely from his/her parents. So, while you may have said or done things in the past that caused your little one to question his/her identity somehow, now is the time to believe in yourself.

We understand how challenging this may be, as having a sick child is humbling and for some, embarrassing. But now, more than ever, you need to believe that God made you a beautiful and wonderful creation, so that you might help to instill confidence and life back into your son or daughter.

In order to do this, first seek healing for yourself. Ask God to show you where your identity has been broken, fragmented or bruised, and invite Him to work in your life to create a confident, caring, loving person who can then serve his/her family.

Following are some traits that contribute to eating-disordered children, and from which God longs to deliver you.

Ego

As my father admitted earlier, passive or aggressive pride can severely damage one's children, for pride prevents one from becoming like a child, and it is only within that position that one can truly love and understand a little one.

If a child does not feel understood, he/she begins to question him/herself, and wonder if he/she is valuable at all. No matter how many times a parent insists "I love you," it's in taking the time to know someone that love is felt.

From the moment a child is born, everything seems strange save for family. Children are learning and absorbing new and wonderful and intimidating facts and faces on a daily basis.

It's crucial, therefore, to keep *your* face, as a parent, close and familiar. Make yours a welcome presence in your child's life by allowing yourself to become accessible. Reach down and hug your child as much as possible; sit down and play Legos or dolls or draw a picture with your little one; slow down so you might hear your child's whisper, his/her cries for help, and his/her craving to be nurtured and needed.

Asceticism

In today's affluent North American culture, many believers struggle with materialism and excess pleasure.

Then there are those that go to the other extreme in order to escape the ways of this world—the ascetics—-who believe in self-denial and strict restraint.

This term defines my father. He is the kind to salvage any piece of food in spite of mold, to hoard bits of rope and wire, to wash cling wrap and reuse it, to wear long johns until they literally fall apart, to buy second-hand purple slippers, to make milk out of skim powder, and to duct tape cardboard to the van window when it breaks.

This would be fine, except that his wife and children were forced into the same lifestyle. Being British, and frugal, my mum easily adapted, for her father had been the same way. Every week she cooked up Saturday Stew, a conglomeration of the week's leftovers mixed together, so as not to waste. She reused tea bags at least twice and insisted the family eat homemade granola every day except Christmas, when we were allowed small boxes of cereal. Orange juice was regulated to half a glass each day.

My parents wore hand-me-downs from Salvation Army, and bought us hand-me-downs for Christmas and birthdays.

(To be fair, we were poor. And while my parents attempted to be wise with their income, they also "splurged" frequently on Sundays after church, when they'd stop by Baker's Dozen Bakery and buy a bag of day-old donuts. These treasured acts were not lost on us.)

When one is in ministry, as my dad was, and living below the poverty line, it's common to set high standards for oneself in the name of "resourcefulness," and to become a martyr for the cause. But no child wants to be dragged into his parent's "righteous cause."

In a twisted sense, I used my parents' asceticism against them, proving that self-denial was in fact, deadly and destructive. Embarrassed by my father's purple shoes and the duct-taped Voyager van; angry that I was forced to drink skim milk powder and eat granola every morning, I rebelled, refusing to partake in my parents' guidelines and setting my own, stricter set of rules to combat them.

And so, considering this, I urge you to re-evaluate your lifestyle.

Do you live to an extreme? If so, ask God to help you balance your indulgences in regards to eating and spending.

If you tend towards asceticism, challenge yourself by asking why you need to be so self-denying. What are you afraid of? Then, dare to let go and trust God when you throw away that piece of rope.

If it's hedonism (excessive pleasure) you struggle with, again, ask yourself why you feel the need so much. The physical, in fact, can keep us from experiencing the spiritual.

Finally, find someone to keep you accountable as you strive for a balanced lifestyle, so you might be a positive example of moderation for your offspring.

Low Self-esteem

My mother struggled with low self-esteem, and her children knew this. She blushed fierce whenever Dad tried to kiss her in public and pushed him away for fear someone would see.

Being an Englishwoman, she was very proper and insisted on changing in her bedroom closet so Dad could not see. She wore shirts that buttoned high to the neck, skirts and pants whose hems brushed the floor, and "skorts" instead of shorts, encouraging her children to do the same.

The birds and the bees were not discussed; rather, they were slid under our bedroom doors through the form of a book. And jealousy was a frequent visitor, as Dad put parishioners' needs before those of his wife and children.

Your children are watching you, observing how you respond to life, to people, and to situations. They see you for who you truly are.

Learn to love yourself. Ask God for the strength to let go of old baggage, to refuse anything the enemy might be whispering into your ear and to believe—to truly, utterly, believe—that you are valuable. *Just as you are.*

Then, you will shine, emanating the beauty of a confident and content spirit.

High Expectations

While Mum battled low self-esteem, Dad fostered high expectations of both his wife and family. He expected that, in public, his family would wear suits and dresses, plaster on smiles, and stay silent. Without a healthy outlet, both wife and children felt smothered by a role they hadn't chosen: that of a pastor's family.

This false front made it painful for my parents to admit to outsiders that they needed help when I became ill; by doing so, they were admitting their "Dr. James Dobson" form of parenting wasn't working, and their happy-go-lucky faces were in fact, masks.

It seems we've forgotten that Jesus came for the sick and the dying. He came to seek the lost sheep, not the flock dressed in pressed suits and pantyhose.

So, check your expectations at the door; they may be subconscious, but your children will sense them. Submit those expectations to God, asking Him to forgive you, humble you, and help you accept your family the way it is, versus the way you think it should be. Then, and only then, will your offspring be free to flourish in their God-given identities.

Poor Communication

Raised in a family in which his mother was seen and not heard, it took years for my father to recognize his wife had a voice.

Thus, when it came to talking about heart-felt matters such as their child's anorexia, both of my parents remained silent in the beginning, believing it best to swallow one's thoughts and continue as if all was normal.

Yet communication, as the next chapter addresses, is the key to establishing a healthy relationship with each other and with one's children. And children long to see their parents happy.

So re-evaluate your connection with your spouse; take time to come before the Lord, together, asking Him to heal your marriage—whichever parts may be scarred or hurting. Unveil secrets to one another, and care deeply about the other. Only then, as a united front, can you properly steer the ship that is your family.

A Parent's Role

Have Healthy, Happy Children

Give your children the freedom to make small yet definite choices. Areas in which they can be shown lenience include dishing up food, choosing what they will wear, and selecting their own hobbies.

- Allow them to make mistakes. Only then will they learn.
- Don't demand; discuss—particularly in the areas of faith, friends and entertainment (TV, Play Station, and the computer). This will keep your children from feeling the need to rebel, because they'll know that you respect them and their opinions, in spite of their youth.
- Don't base your parenting style on someone else's; instead, base it on the wisdom God gives you.
- Don't keep a weigh scale or an unnecessary amount of mirrors or fashion magazines in your house.
- Don't make comments about people's size or weight. Instead, remark on attributes that you hope will shine through your own children: character, integrity, and other facets of inner beauty.
- Look your children in the eyes when they are talking to you, and reiterate what they are saying to help them feel validated and listened to.
- Compliment and encourage your children on a regular basis. Mothers, remind your husbands and sons to affirm your daughters.
- Know your child's love language, be it gifts, words of affirmation, acts of service, quality time, or physical touch. Make an effort to demonstrate this particular form of love each day.
- Let your children be children. Don't give them more chores than necessary; encourage play as well as work.
- Be available. Make time to play with your children.
- Have an open-door policy when it comes to bedrooms.
- Pray for your little ones daily, that God's Spirit would guide their decisions, and that angels would protect their minds and

their hearts.
• Teach your children that God's love is a gift, not an obligation.
• Consider the uniqueness of each child; recognize his/her gifts and encourage them, accordingly.
• Finally, exert healthy self-confidence. Avoid talking negatively about yourself, and teach your children to believe in themselves.

Love Your Sick Child

• Pray for healing for your child on a daily, even hourly, basis.
• Pray for wisdom, that God would guide you as a parent and give you humility, understanding and unending patience.
• Apologize to your child (for the ways you've tried to control him in the past; for the ways in which you've hurt him; for forcing him to grow up too fast; for refusing to acknowledge or encourage him; for not listening to him); then, ask for forgiveness.
• Consider the roots of the illness: What factors triggered it? What is your child trying to say to you? How can you help your child feel "in control" of her own life? How can you support her during this time, without making her feel threatened?
• Recognize your child's gifts and talents, and encourage him in those (in the hopes that he will begin to find his identity in something other than the ED).
• Keep in mind, your child doesn't want help; he wants hope—hope that one day, things won't be this hard; hope that one day, you will be his friend and you will understand.\
• As hard as it is to watch your child refuse to eat, don't try to fix the illness unless it's life-threatening. Rather, try to get to know your son/daughter again. Work on re-establishing that relationship and tearing down walls. The problem, most likely, lies in years of feeling abandoned and out of control (eating disorders are often the result of a deep hurt, and stem from not wanting to get hurt again).
• Keep all talk regarding your own appearance and that of others' positive and uplifting. Avoid discussing body size, weight, or calories.

Love Your Other Children

No matter how acute your child's condition; no matter the signs that prove she is struggling with eating, it is essential not to forget your other children. This will no doubt be challenging, as your ill child demands attention on a consistent basis; but if the others are ignored, they, too, will begin to take extreme measures in order to be noticed.

Make Mealtimes Merry

Eating together at least once a day provides the opportunity for holy interaction; it solidifies a family, opening up hearts around food and using the sharing of plate and cup to unify. Food is meant for the coming-together of believers, for communion. God designed it to be so. He desires fellowship across the tablecloth.

Eating disorders rob a family of this meal-time unity. They destroy the peacefulness of gathering together—the beauty of being one—and make each family member yearn for solitude.

God is present in the gathering of His people. Satan delights in dividing. This, I believe, is one of his key goals through eating disorders—to steal away the sanctuary of mealtime.

Mealtimes are tricky. Knowing when to respond, and when to stay quiet, requires prayer. When a child is refusing to eat at the table, thereby disturbing the harmony and causing siblings to worry about calories and whether or not they, too, are "fat," parents may either a) make too big a deal of it, and catalyze regular fights at the dinner table, or b) try to ignore the matter altogether in an attempt to treat each child fairly.

It is important to understand that children know when something is wrong. Children are often wise beyond their years, and are desperate for two things: affirmation and knowledge. Constantly learning, they wonder why their sibling—who in many cases may be the older one—is refusing to eat, and when did food become bad?

As much as it might pain you, make an effort to keep mealtimes light and fun. You can address your child's refusal to eat following the meal, but don't make it a bigger issue than it needs to be. Rather, acknowledge the difficulty, then focus hard on the other children, asking about their day, what might have made them smile, and what upset them.

Make it your goal to get to know your children over steaming plates of food. Make an effort to smile and speak in loving, quiet tones, no matter the anxiety of your heart. And God will bless you for walking so, in faith. He will mend broken hearts and will heal your family, in His timing. By trusting this, and by acting in prayerful love for your other children, you will find reward.

Talk About It

I'd like to urge you, as parents, to use this painful situation to communicate freely with each child; to teach your family about the eating disorder and to hide nothing, for in hiding, one merely creates tension and bitterness.

My family held monthly meetings in which my father sketched out the budget on an easel and asked if anyone had questions. While this was good, I longed for him to simply set down the calculator, crouch to my level, and see my tear-filled eyes.

There was an elephant in the room that could not be ignored, yet somehow, he and my mum managed to. They pretended nothing was wrong. But something was. And the elephant only grew larger (or thinner, as one might want to look at it) the longer it was ignored.

Be honest with your children. Talk about the issue at bedtime, one-on-one with your offspring. Talk about it as you drive them to soccer practice or swimming lessons. Take them out for cinnamon buns, as my dad did in later years. Most parents don't want to admit they don't know something; they don't want to appear weak in front of their children, but remember, God is present in our weakness.

With this in mind, admit to your children when you are/have been wrong. Go to the Lord, seeking truth about your situation and what you need to ask forgiveness for. Then, confess your sins to your children. It will help them to know that you, too, are scared; that you, too, are human. But that God is still God, and He is still very much in control.

Keep 'em Young

Your other children are witnessing a very mature issue at a young age; eating disorders force young people to grow up fast.

Do everything you can to keep them young. Sing to them. Tell jokes even when the air is taut with tension, and spend time making crafts, eating ice cream, playing in parks, dancing long dances and dreaming big dreams. Read stories to them and help them develop the colors of their imagination in a house black with suffering.

And most importantly, love them.

Affirm and Educate

As mentioned earlier, children yearn for affirmation and education. Keeping this in mind, make an effort to compliment each of them sincerely, every day. This will take a lot of strength and vision, to see past your own pain to the beauty of the people around you, but as their faces light up, you will realize—it pays to notice.

Ask God for His eyes, to truly see your children and to give you a heart for each of them, as you may be feeling sapped dry by your ill child. Ask the Lord to overflow you with strength, so you might invest in each of your family members. And ask Him for wisdom to know how to best guide your family into a healing place.

Part of this healing can come through learning together. Borrow books from the library on eating disorders. Rent DVDs. Educate yourselves and your children. Don't leave them in the dark. You are all suffering. Use this time to bond together—not against the disordered eater, but *for* him or her.

Inspire Compassion

It may feel as though your child is out to "get you"—that he/she is choosing each day to enter into fits of rage and obstinacy. And in some ways, he/she is. But deep down, the intent is not to hurt you. Deep down, he/she is battling feelings and thoughts he/she doesn't really understand.

As hard as it may be to believe, eating disorders are a mental illness, and even the initial stages need to be treated seriously. With this in mind, counsel your children to treat it similarly. Protect your sick child by upholding his/her name in front of the others. Do not commend the way he/she is acting, but explain that this is an illness that needs to be treated with compassion and love.

Healing cannot come about in any other way. Urge your children to their knees on behalf of their sibling. And, particularly following a big fight, call the others together and pray on your child's behalf, using prayer for no means other than to beseech the heart of God.

Chapter 3

Siblings' Perspective

Keith's Story

HE WORE HIS FAVORITE Blue Jays T-shirt. He sat on his bedroom floor, surrounded by Legos, sketching. He could hear her, downstairs, screaming. Could hear her calling names, crying; his mum slamming pots and pans and his dad, speaking in a strained voice.

Now, she was running upstairs. The girl he no longer knew. The girl that used to be his best friend. His pencil snapped in two.

Down the hall, he knew his sisters would be huddled in their room, praying. He didn't understand how they could pray. Looking down at his picture, he sighed.

Then, when the house was quiet, when his parents and siblings had fallen asleep, Keith slipped downstairs and taped it to the refrigerator door. The picture of his older sister as a wrecking ball, destroying the wall of his family.

***

"I regretted having drawn it, but at the same time it accurately depicted how I felt at the time," the father of three now admits.

Until Emily developed anorexia, she and Keith had been thick as thieves. Just 17 months apart, they'd spent their first year together in Africa, where their parents were missionaries. They hunted snakes together, bathed outdoors in buckets under the hot African sun, chased stray cats and played dress-up.

Even after Allison and Meredith joined the family back in Canada, Keith and Emily shared a solid bond, making mud pies in the sandbox, building snowmen, creating costumes and playing games long after their siblings went to sleep.

Yet as Emily grew, her attention began to shift. And when she left her home-schooling siblings and started attending public school, the great divide occurred. She started to spend more time in front of the mirror and less time with her family. She started locking herself in the bathroom and standing on the scale. Keith, in turn, hid in his room reading the Hardy Boys. And he became angry at the girl who'd upset his world just because she didn't want to eat.

"It made her the center-point of the family," Keith states. "Instead of focusing on what we could be doing together, we were focusing on what she *wasn't* doing."

He couldn't understand why his older sister cared so much about what she looked like, and why she would rather hurt herself than play with him. And he couldn't rationalize why she needed to upset the entire family.

"I just didn't understand why she wouldn't eat, especially seeing how it hurt Dad and Mum," says the 30-year-old recruitment and employee relations specialist. "I became angry at her stubbornness and defiance."

At times, in his anger, Keith would call Emily a skeleton, just to see her react. And she'd fly into a preadolescent rage, screaming at the brother she'd once called friend.

It was all he knew to do, however, to show how she'd hurt him. Anger was the easiest way to deal with the situation without thinking about it too much. If he thought about it, Keith might start to miss Emily, and he couldn't let himself do that, for that would demonstrate weakness.

As a family, they didn't talk about the eating disorder. Instead, everyone just watched in silence as Emily slammed doors and threw things. They listened to her sobbing within her bedroom, and turned away, not knowing how to communicate with each other or with her.

Being the only boy in the family, Keith felt he should stand up for his parents and defend them when Emily tried to hurt them, both verbally and physically.

"I wished she would get over herself and realize what it was doing to the family," he says.

Allison's Story

Allison, the middle sibling, felt distant and unappreciated, "like Emily didn't want a sister," the 28-year-old admits. "I felt rejected, as if I wasn't good enough to be her friend, or someone she could talk to or be interested in."

At the same time, she desired to let Emily know how much she cared about her. "I understood it wasn't easy being a kid, or being treated like one," Allison says. "And I hoped she felt loved soon."

Her oldest sister had changed seemingly overnight, into a person who was forever tired, anxious, tense, angry, bitter, resentful, ashamed of her family, and depressed.

"When Mum started telling Emily to eat the rest of what was on her plate, then I picked up on the fact that she didn't want to eat at all," says Allison, who was six at the time. "It took some time before I realized that it went to her heart, though, and the way she felt about herself and her life, as if something significant was not right."

As her sister's anorexic symptoms intensified, Allison says, "I felt an ache, like she was on a raft, drifting farther away from us, and although I was scared she was going far away, God didn't let us lose hope completely that she would, someday, maybe choose to come back.

"I think Meredith and I talked about this a lot, or at least that we were scared but knew God was the one who could speak to Emily's heart even if she didn't know how much we cared. It was pretty evident that He would have to convince her to choose life and His love, because it seemed like there was a huge wall up (literally and emotionally) between her and the rest of us.

"I wanted to tell her that it would be okay, and that she could rest, and just forget about what everybody else says, knowing that she was loved. I hoped God would show her, somehow, where all the love she was missing was, all along. We just didn't know how to communicate it, especially while she was hurting."

Allison recalls having a dream in which Emily let herself be hugged. "I told Meredith about it," she says, "and prayed that it would happen someday."

Meredith's Story

Emily's youngest sister experienced more sadness than anger. "All I knew was that she wasn't eating, and that there were a lot of fights about something or other between her, Mum and Dad," says 26-

year-old Meredith, currently obtaining her master's in counseling. "I was sad that there was so much fighting. I was worried about Emily, and felt bad for Mum and Dad."

Meredith recalls trying to fall asleep while Emily yelled in the kitchen below her bedroom. "Then, after Emily went to her room, I would hear pots, pans, cupboard doors and the stove drawer slamming as Mum and Dad continued to argue the matter."

Every time Emily slammed her door, Meredith prayed fervently, for she'd read a youth devotional that dealt with suicide. "I was in intense fear that she was going to kill herself," Meredith says. "I prayed for her a lot at that time, whenever I was scared for her life."

Despite being just four years old when Emily became anorexic, Meredith admits to having felt fat. "Rather than comparing my body with Emily's, however, I would often compare it with friends' who were the same age as me," she says. "I can't remember a time when I didn't think I was too large."

Nevertheless, Meredith tried to eat more in order to compensate for Emily's empty plate "so that people wouldn't worry I was also anorexic," she explains. "At church potlucks I would heap food on my plate that I didn't even want to eat. I didn't feel like I could eat healthily or cut down on anything, because that would be alarming. Even exercising was something I did tentatively because I didn't want it to be taken the wrong way."

She felt pressured, even at such a young age, to play mediator within her broken family. "By my silence, I tried to keep the peace," Meredith says.

Yet in spite of everything—in spite of the fear, the sadness and the sleepless nights—Meredith was in awe of her oldest sister, who stood up for her and gave her a voice. "I wanted to spend more time with her, but appreciated everything that she did for me."

A Sibling's Role

It is difficult to watch your brother or sister refuse to eat on a daily basis. You're no doubt wondering what happened to make him/her so sad; perhaps you're blaming yourself, thinking it must have been something you did or didn't do.

Perhaps you're angry, hiding out in your room, drawing pictures of your sibling as a wrecking ball. Or maybe you're trying to play mediator, keeping the peace amongst everyone while crying on the inside.

Please know, first of all, that *you are not to blame.* Your brother/sister loves you, and his/her sickness has nothing to do with you.

Please also know that your sister's or brother's recovery does not depend on you. Breathe deep, and relax. This, too, shall pass. In the meantime, what you say and do *will* make a difference in your hurting sibling's life. Here are some tips:

- **Speak in love.** No matter how you feel, say everything in love. For example, even when your sick sibling yells at you, swallow your pride, and breathe in and out for a few moments before responding; or, if need be, walk away so you don't say anything hurtful. Keep in mind, while your sibling is being hurtful, it's the illness talking, not the person you know and love. So, like the adage goes, if you can't say anything nice, don't say anything at all.
- **Pray fervently.** Your prayers will be heard, so pray fervently and often. And if you don't know what to say, just sit quietly before the cross and God will see your heart and bless it.
- **Don't stop believing.** God hasn't changed. He is, and forever will be, faithful and loving. And He is working, even now, to redeem your sibling's life. Don't give up. And don't lose faith.
- **Don't question yourself.** Just because your sibling doubts him/herself, doesn't mean that you need to. You are a unique creation whom God put on this planet for His special purposes, one of which is to love this person who is hurting.
- **Seek an outlet.** Vent your frustrations, questions and sadness through sports, poetry, painting or music.
- **Make a mentor-friend.** Find an adult whom you trust outside of the home, and spend time talking and praying together. This person will give you perspective, as well as the attention you're no doubt craving.

• **Spend time with your siblings,** building them up, encouraging them, and even suffering together on behalf of the one who is hurting. They need you. And you need them. There is power in unity.

Chapter 4
Professional Perspective

The Doctor's Diagnosis

DENA CABRERA, Psy.D., Clinical Director of Adolescent Services at Rosewood's Centers for Eating Disorders and former psychologist at Arizona's Remuda Ranch, has not only dealt with eating disorders for the past two decades, but has been instrumental in developing a program for patients with acute anorexia nervosa. She believes eating disorders can be traced, to an extent, to one's genetics.

"Anorexia is a complex disorder with multiple triggers and influencing factors," she says. "There is a significant role genetic factors play into the development of anorexia. There is not one gene for anorexia or one gene for bulimia but instead, there is a host of genes that code for proteins which influence traits that make one vulnerable to this disorder."

Such traits include low self-esteem, perfectionism, need for exact order, harm avoidance and anxiety. Yet one's environment, Cabrera says, also figures into the disease, taking into account the following factors:

• Family attitudes and behaviors regarding food, including parental modeling of thinness, weight, and shape issues.
• Parents' *non-verbal and verbal* responses to their bodies and child's body.
• Familial history of being overweight or on a diet.
• Perceived parental pressure to be slender and to control weight/shape.
• General family function (Competitive? Communicative?).
• Physical contact (i.e., affection, boundaries, verbal and non-verbal expression of love).
• Peer influences—dieting, weight talk, teasing.
• Psychiatric/psychological issues—anxiety (which almost al-

ways precedes the onset of an eating disorder), depression, lack of resilience, emotional deregulation (which is at the core of eating disorders, trauma, and substance abuse issues).
• Body image dissatisfaction (over-evaluation of weight and shape which drives the eating disorder behaviors).
• Socio-cultural influences, such as unrealistic standards of beauty portrayed by media.

Diagnostic Criteria

When diagnosing a disordered eater, Cabrera follows the DSM-IV diagnostic criteria of mental disorders, consisting of:

• **Refusal to maintain body weight** at or above a minimally normal weight for age and height (i.e., weight loss leading to maintenance of body weight less than 85 percent of that expected; or failure to make expected weight gain during period of growth, leading to body weight less than 85 percent of that expected).
• **Intense fear of gaining weight** or becoming fat, even though underweight.
• **Disturbance in the way one's body weight or shape is experienced**, undue influence of body weight or shape on self-evaluation, or denial of the seriousness of the current low body weight.
• **In post-menarcheal females, amenorrhea**; i.e., the absence of at least three consecutive menstrual cycles. (A woman is considered to have amenorrhea if her period occurs only following hormones, i.e., estrogen administration.)

Helpful Tips

Upon recognizing the symptoms of an eating disorder in one's child, Cabrera recommends taking the following steps:

• Learn all you can about eating disorders.
• Don't expect your child to acknowledge the problem or em-

brace your help. He may feel extremely threatened by the thought of giving up the dysfunctional eating behavior.

• Don't believe your child's claim that he does not need professional help.

• Obtain treatment for your child.

• Seek help only from healthcare professionals/facilities that specialize in eating disorders.

• Be patient. Treatment takes time; recovery may take months or years and involve relapses.

• Participate in family therapy as recommended by treatment providers.

• In conflicts about decisions, do not retreat from your position for fear that your child will become more ill. Your child needs clear, kind, and decisive communication.

• Maintain a supportive, confident, hopeful posture.

• Express honest affection verbally and physically; your child needs to know that he is loved.

• Talk with your child about personal issues other than food and weight.

• Do not demand weight gain or berate your child for having an eating disorder.

• Do not become your child's policeman. If you see a change in your child's weight or behavior, call his counselor or physician.

• Expect your child to be responsible for her actions by replacing food that was binged on and cleaning up messes (bathroom, kitchen, etc.).

• Expect your child to be with the family during mealtimes, but do not demand that he eat.

• Do not let your child decide what the family eats for dinner. Do not allow his eating disorder to dominate the family's eating schedule or use of the kitchen. Do not allow him to shop or cook for the family.

• Do not make mealtime a battle of wills.

• Do not watch the person when eating, or make comments about food.

• Do not apologize for or make excuses for the person's eating habits.

• Do not play nutritionist. Do not give detailed food or nutrition-related advice. Model and talk about balance and moderation.

• Do not read your child's journal.

• Do not exaggerate for effect, saying, "Your illness is damaging the whole family... I can't take much more of this." Catastrophic statements will only exacerbate the eating disorder behavior.

• Do not say, "Help me to help you!" or "What can I do for you?" These statements suggest that the child knows what he needs to heal from the eating disorder, when he does not.

• Do not allow your child to disrupt your life through manipulation, arguments, threats, blame, guilt, bribes, or resentment.

• Do not feel guilty or waste time figuring out the cause of the eating disorder or assigning blame. Remember that families neither cause nor cure eating disorders.

• Do not try to protect your child from the natural consequences of an eating disorder. The pain it causes your child and others will (hopefully) motivate recovery.

• Be limitless in supporting and encouraging every hint of recovery that you see.

• Do not put your child's needs before your own. Do not exhaust yourself. Take care of yourself for the long journey of recovery, modeling balance and health.

• Pray and trust God for the outcome.

The Counselor's Case

Power struggles concerning food or body weight are strong indicators of a problem, says Len Thompson, B.R.A., M.A., the former director of Northern Christian Counseling Services in Sault Ste. Marie, Ontario, and one of three professionals involved in Emily's diagnosis.

Spiritually, these power struggles suggest something has gone wrong in the formation of the child's concept of personal identity. "Satan provides alluring lies to the [disordered eater], that control of power is the perfect solution to their perceived loss of legitimate autonomy, rather than a loving relationship of trust with Christ," Thompson says.

This "control of power" can manifest itself through monitoring body weight, food intake, family dynamics, exercise, and depending on others' perceptions and emotions to compensate for a validated sense of identity.

Spiritually Speaking

God desires for each of His creations to develop a healthy ability to make choices, express desires and preferences, as well as feel and think independently, Thompson states, so we might reflect His image.

Satan desires, in turn, to rob God's creation of these abilities, providing "an almost irresistible substitute for true identity—power."

To combat Satan's attempts, Thompson encourages parents to adopt the parenting style of God the Father. "He always gives us choices even if He doesn't like the choices we make. He affirms our creativity and encourages self-expression. He is always ready to hear our concerns, disappointments and pain."

God never tries to steal His children's identity. In the same way, Thompson says, parents should try to allow for an honest expression of their child's personality—as much as it might hurt them. This acceptance is what a child craves; this kind of unconditional love.

Small Steps

While meeting with Emily and her parents, Thompson recalls little advances proved to be giant landmarks. These milestones included allowing Emily to decorate her room, letting her choose which television program she wanted to watch (as negotiated by her mum and dad), writing in her diary or journal without either parent reading it, and purchasing her own clothes versus putting up with hand-me-downs.

"It is very important for parents to consider how their child's identity is faring in the transition from childhood to adulthood," he says.

Issues at Hand

In the midst of striving to love one's eating-disordered child, Thompson warns that issues can arise, hindering a parent's advancement. For example, one might feel powerless to give his/her child choices in light of the needs of other family members.

"Sometimes the health of someone else in the family might take center-stage, but a parent must find creative ways to enlist the community's help to make sure that each child gets emotional attention," he says.

Another issue Thompson has observed is that of feeling powerless to give one's ill child choices due to the pressure of serving God. "God *does* ask for our sacrifices," he says, "but never at the expense of our children's identities."

No matter a person's ministerial position, there is no excuse for one's family to be exploited by way of monetary neglect, verbal abuse from parishioners or malicious gossip.

"I'd like to empower parents to act *for* their children rather than feeling obligated to sacrifice them."

Satan, says Thompson, is very active in this regard—twisting efforts made in the name of ministry. "There are times when leaving an organization or a church is the right thing to do for the sake of your children, and there is nothing to feel guilty about in that situation."

Parents also sometimes feel powerless to connect with their eating-disordered child, due to guilt over their young one's situation. While repentance may be needed for some choices a parent has made, the child's anger stems not from blaming the parent, but from the authority figure which the parent represents.

"I can remember telling Emily's parents to be patient," says Thompson, "and not to doubt that Emily loved them, but I think they thought I was making that up because she sometimes told them how angry she was."

Yet, the fact that Emily was willing to share her anger with her parents showed that she entrusted them with her feelings—negative as they were—and this was, indeed, a positive sign.

Thompson recalls urging Ernest to connect with Emily through notes, father-daughter dates and conversations. "It took a lot for both to believe the relationship could be redeemed," he recalls. "I spent a fair bit of time encouraging them and reminding them that God was still working."

Because He is, Thompson says. Working. Even when a child is screaming in his parents' faces, cursing the day they were born; even when a plate of food slams into a wall and both parent and child run to their bedrooms weeping, God is working.

Yet the strain can become too much—the anger and grief too trying—resulting in parents feeling powerless to connect with God. "It can be invaluable for parents to seek deep, soul conversations with godly people who can help them with their despair," stresses Thompson. "God weeps over the damage done by an eating disorder, and often parents need someone to weep with them."

It is essential, he adds, for parents and siblings to demonstrate care for one another during this time, for it is through this love that God's presence can be felt. "We don't know what God is up to, but if we learn to listen, the relationship with God can be restored and we can hear Him speak."

Love is the Answer

To prevent the illness from spreading further, Thompson encourages families to focus on loving the individual versus analyzing food intake or calories. "Showing a disordered eater that he/she is valuable is so important. Express love constantly; listen to the heart, and validate identity."

By doing so, the child will have less reason to express his/her anger through starvation. "Constant reminders of love weaken Satan's power."

Listening Prayer

And finally, instead of preaching at one's child, Thompson suggests the spiritual exercise of listening prayer. "If we can hear God communicate the specific thing that needs to be done each day, what could be more important?" he says. "Prayer that allows us to see through God's eyes is much different from prayer that demands God do what we think is best."

Chapter 5

Prayer

Dear Heavenly Father,
THANK YOU FOR BEING here with us. Thank You for loving our family and for desiring wholeness, healing and well-being for each one of us. Thank You for sending Your Son to die on our behalf; we'll never understand the pain You must have felt.

Yet we know pain, nonetheless, and ask that You strengthen us now.

Forgive us, LORD, for whatever role we may have played in the development of this eating disorder. Forgive us for thinking we know what's best for _____, and help us to trust that You are in control. Forgive us for holding onto guilt, and help us to have faith that even now, You are rescuing _____ from the grip of (anorexia, bulimia, binge eating, compulsive over-eating, etcetera).

Give us faith to believe, in spite of our pain. Give us hope, in spite of the darkness. Show us how You are working in _____'s life, and what You desire of us as parents, siblings and friends. Give us Your wisdom, LORD. Give us faith to see through Your eyes.

We know we can do nothing apart from You. Give us grace today, LORD, to be loving parents, siblings and friends. Help us to see a person instead of a patient. Help us to love _____ the way he/she needs to be loved.

We commit _____ to You now, and surrender all of the factors that led to him/her developing this illness. We ask that he/she would feel Your embrace right now; that ___ would know he/she is beautifully and wonderfully made. Give us wisdom to know how to convey this truth to _____ on a daily basis.

We come against the enemy in Jesus' name, and bind any spirits that may be whispering lies to _____. We ask that You would release our child/sibling/friend from those lies, and reveal the truth to him/her.

Speak to _____ through dreams, word and deed. Show Your love to him/her and peel the blinders from his/her eyes. Help food take its rightful place in the life of ____, and help us to not focus on weight or exercise, but instead, on being agents of love.

We have observed the symptoms of an eating disorder in our child/sibling/friend, LORD, but we know that You are bigger than it, and that through You, our loved one's life can be redeemed. Use us, this day, we pray, to be Your vessels.

We wait, and hope, humbled at the foot of the cross.

Amen.

Part II

REACTING

*What to do when
the disorder gets worse*

Chapter 6

Child's Perspective

My Story

I HAD ALWAYS BEEN gentle-mannered and obedient, polite and sweet. But the less I ate, the angrier I became. It was as though starvation was the key to a room full of pent-up feelings.

Eventually I turned into a shadow of my former self. My eating disorder gave me an alternate identity; I felt like I could do anything because of it. I thrived on the feeling of power; on having people listen to me when I yelled; on believing I was beautiful because I weighed less.

I hungered for control. I spent hours in front of the bathroom mirror, sucking in my cheeks, loving the way my hip bones jutted out. Every night before falling asleep I listened to my stomach gurgle and groan—much like a pregnant woman with a baby moving inside her—only mine was a sick pleasure.

Every night I wrapped my fingers around my wrists and measured myself, determined to stay small. And every night I planned out the next day's meals.

Losing Control

For the most part, starvation wasn't about losing weight. It was about not gaining any—but if I lost some, I felt more in control. The more I lost, the safer I felt.

Health meant nothing. Size was everything. To be healthy was to be plump. I wanted to look sick and haunted. I liked the angular edge of my bones. And the skinnier I became, the more beautiful I felt.

For a long time, I didn't admit to being anorexic; in fact, I insisted I wasn't. I merely thought I was being disciplined, that I was choosing to be thin, and that my family should support me in this newfound mission. Anyone who didn't support me was the enemy.

With anorexia rose a fierce and competitive spirit. I wanted to dominate the household, but felt threatened by my father. I grew to despise the quiet way in which he controlled the home, and began to lash out physically against him, trying to make him loosen his grip.

Mealtimes were tense, as I cut down further and further on serving sizes. Breakfast was half a piece of bread. Lunch, the same thing, and supper, anything I wanted, because I'd earned it by not eating much at the other meals.

Then, I began to insist on eating only one of something at supper—whether it be tapioca, cheese, or bread. I'd eat as much as I wanted, but only *one thing*. Later, I began to monitor how much of that one thing I consumed, until I was only eating a tiny serving. Each day fluctuated, monitored by the weigh scales I used after every meal.

I had never been an athletic girl, but when I learned how many calories could be burned off by running, I began to jog around the house each evening. I also took up skipping rope. I didn't know how ridiculous I looked, a bony girl seeming much like an old woman, feebly running and skipping. I felt powerful inside. Invincible. Death was not an option. I could live on next to nothing. Everyone had been wrong; food wasn't necessary. It was merely an indulgence.

Summers were spent in northern Ontario at a cottage by Caufield Lake. Each night, my stomach could be heard through the thin partitions of plywood, growling long into the dawn. I found joy in these growls, knowing I'd eaten little that day.

Days were filled with screams and slamming doors.

And then, I stopped hugging my parents altogether. For the next few years we lived estranged lives. I would cry in my dreams, imagining my mother's arms around me, holding me. I missed feeling loved, but love had become a weakness. I couldn't afford to be weak, for that might make me slip up and eat. And that would be unforgivable.

Baptized at the age of eight into my dad's church, I believed in the existence of God, and knew I was created to have a personal relationship with Him. Yet He wasn't real to me. It was all head knowledge. And, as I dabbled in the anorexic occult, my faith became nothing more than a precarious piece in the puzzle that was my life—

-just another element to be controlled.

I had no strength to care for anyone. My thoughts were completely absorbed by ever-counting calories. If I stopped planning my skinny-strategy for even a moment, I might give in, and so, I never stopped. And for all I knew, my prayers were merely bouncing off the ceiling back into my bedroom.

In spite of being controlled, I was convinced I was still in control. And I thrived on this, in a strict, regimented family. Anything that threatened this sense of control caused me to lose my temper.

My parents began to make efforts to help me. They hired Christian counselors who annoyed me with their soft voices and quiet, religious demeanors. I was polite to them, but didn't listen, for they were pawns of my parents. They had never known what it was like to starve for attention.

I didn't trust anyone who couldn't understand or support my mission to refuse food. They tried to give me a "voice" through television privileges and an allowance. But it was too late. I had already found my voice through anorexia.

Then came the summer of 1991, when Mum and Dad announced they were taking me to the Hospital for Sick Children (SickKids) in Toronto. At 11 years old, I was forced into a drafty hospital gown, shoved into a room on the psych ward, given a tray full of food, and told to eat by the end of the week or I wouldn't be allowed to return home.

I curled into a bony ball on my bed, and listened to the patients making strange noises outside my door. My family left to do the tourist thing, and I remained, planning my escape. I would eat, but only on the last day, so I could get out. Then, I'd cut back even more. For no one could control me. I'd show them. I was not sick, and I did not need help.

And so that is what I did. On the very last day, one week after being admitted, I ate, and everyone rejoiced.

But I knew better. Even as we drove home, I was scheduling the next week's meals in my mind. Sitting stonily in the back seat, desperate to prove I was still in control.

Knowing deep down, I wasn't.

Personally Speaking

I wasn't ready to get better. I hadn't even realized I was sick. It would take another two years of starving myself before I'd hit rock bottom.

An eating disorder is a mental illness. It is a distortion of the very way in which we see society, ourselves, and our loved ones. It is not something that can be cured by a physical solution, such as sticking a child in a hospital and shoving a plate of food under his/her nose. I understand why my parents tried this; they got scared. They were afraid I was going to die. But I wasn't. I also wasn't ready to get better, yet. And so, the experience only pushed me to continue not eating.

Food is the tool which disordered eaters use to express their mental illness. Food is not threatening. People are. We know how to manipulate food. We like the concept of food, because it's so moldable. We can dream about it, salivate over it, and then refuse it. We can watch others lift utensils to their mouths and feel full just by thinking about food.

For me, it hadn't yet become a matter of life and death—something it would have to be in order for me to desire change. In a twisted way, I was happy. I had found what I was looking for: my identity. My own way of standing apart from the others. My own way of feeling important. My own way of being in control.

I didn't stop to consider how I was hurting others. For me, obliviousness was a defense mechanism. And anger was a weapon. Being angry kept me from being weak. I had never been angrier, and I had never felt stronger. Being strong kept me from feeling hunger. And, ironically, I fed off hunger. It was proof that I was doing something right.

I was only angry with my family. Outside of home, I was quiet and demure, because outside of home, people weren't threatening. And outside of home, people weren't committed to loving me for the rest of my life. I knew my family would never leave me. I didn't know that about my friends, and, being a people pleaser, it mattered greatly what they thought.

I didn't need to have my guard up outside of the house, because no one knew of my food obsession. They knew I was thin, but they didn't know that it was on purpose. I would choose not to eat at home so I could partake in the snacks at my friend's party the following night. I let myself eat around others, so they wouldn't think me strange. They knew I was skinny, but at this point, it wasn't scary.

I gave no thought to the future. My energy was consumed with planning meals. Every night, as my stomach pleaded, begged and bargained with me, I mentally prepared for the next day until my defenses were set and my battle plan ready. I knew what I was going to wear, weeks ahead of time. I wrote down every detail. My room was immaculately clean. I studied furiously, reading and re-reading what my starved mind found hard to absorb, so I could ace every test.

Eventually, after four years of this power trip, I became tired. So tired that I wondered, *Why bother?* At that point, I began to think about the future. I began to think about high school, about dating, about finding someone to fall in love with. I began to dream of college and what I would become. And I began to realize, *I don't want to do this the rest of my life. It's too exhausting. Will I ever be able to eat again?*

In those moments, I bawled into my pillow, liquid prayers of regret, begging God to make me normal. I wept into wet cotton every night, keeping my angry façade throughout the day.

But I was no longer angry at the people around me. I began to realize they were concerned about me, and to understand why. I wasn't angry at them so much as I was angry at myself. At what I'd gotten myself into. Because, being a perfectionist, I thought I'd have to see this through to completion.

And that scared me, because completion meant death. And I wasn't ready to die.

Chapter 7

Parents' Perspective

Ernest's Story

HER FACE WAS AS purple as an eggplant, her eyes popping red, and she was hitting him—this daughter who once lay cooing in his arms; who he'd sung to sleep under Congo skies; who he'd taught to walk and run and ride a bike.

He didn't recognize her anymore. Who was this girl with the popsicle-stick arms? Her arms were so skinny; too skinny. He hadn't really noticed until now—maybe he hadn't let himself see—how sick she looked.

She was screaming in his face, things like "I hate you," and "You're nothing to me," when all of a sudden he felt himself push her against the wall. He pinned her there, forcing her to stop flailing.

For a moment, she just stared at him, her eyes wide. He didn't even say anything, just held her there against the wall until his heart had stopped racing; then he let her go and she ran to her room, crying, and he crumbled to the floor wondering who *he'd* become and what to do now.

Yvonne's Story

She could hear it through the thin walls, hours after Emily had gone to bed. Emily's stomach, like a caged, snarling animal. Emily went to bed early these days, unable to stay awake for her rigid daily routine—eating only half a slice of bread for breakfast, then exercising, then another half slice of bread for lunch, then more exercise, then a tiny nibble for supper.

Yvonne had hoped they'd be able to relax out here at the cottage; that the sound of the loons and the lap of waves might stir her daughter's heart, make her mellow and happy. But she barely smiled these days, keeping to herself when she wasn't running around the house, while her siblings scavenged the woods and played games in

July twilight.

She couldn't sleep, for the growling. It seemed to be getting worse. Emily hadn't let her hug her for a year now; she ached to hold her little girl. So, slipping in her summer nightgown down the hall, Yvonne arrived at Emily's room, pausing to make sure the stick-like form beneath the sheet was asleep.

Then, Yvonne slid into bed, next to her daughter, tucked arms about her, and smothered a scream. Emily was all bone. There was no flesh, only jagged edges. Hips, ribs, arms, everything. Her baby girl—bone.

For a moment Yvonne lay limp, then she pulled herself away and tip-toed to the living room where she sat by bay windows and cried at the moon. Begging God to show her what to do.

And as morning stretched pink across the lake, she decided: they would take Emily to the hospital.

Weighing in the Factors

Once Yvonne realized Emily had anorexia, she tried everything to convince her daughter to eat: teaspoons of Cod Liver Oil as punishment for not finishing meals; menus; charts; she even tried to diet in a healthy manner to show Emily one could still lose weight while eating nutritiously.

As Emily consumed less and exercised more, her parents began to read up on the subject.

"I hoped it would be a passing phase," Ernest says, "but as time went on, we realized it wouldn't go away on its own."

He admits to feeling helpless. "We kept trusting God and praying He would bring about change where we couldn't."

Even as Emily lashed out at him, "I felt more disappointed," says Ernest. "Everybody else felt sad too, when there was a blow-up (like our dog Christie, we wanted to tuck tail between our legs and go find a refuge).

"I wished I could help her," he admits. "I tried to provide a framework and a routine; reliable expectations that would encourage Emily to 'see the light' and return to normal eating."

Together, he and Yvonne sought counseling, in addition to encouraging and enticing Emily to eat more.

"Our relationship with our daughter seemed distant. There was a wall up between us," Ernest recalls. Yet he continued to trust God, while begging Him to heal Emily.

Both Ernest and Yvonne felt puzzled that things were going wrong when they were trying so hard to do everything right.

"Emily had always been so good," says Yvonne. "But then she didn't have the energy to be good anymore."

Not being allowed to hug her own daughter was the hardest, Yvonne admits. Recalling the night she entered Emily's bedroom and lay down beside her while she slept, "I could feel her hip bones through her clothes, and I cried. That was the day I decided she needed the hospital because we couldn't do anything more for her."

They both regret not having prayed more. "However, we learned to pray as the years passed," says Yvonne. "We prayed for healing for Emily, and understanding for us."

"We realized we weren't ideal parents, and that we needed God's help," Ernest adds. "We needed His help to love Emily more and see her as she was."

Yvonne admits to having felt extremely guilty. "I blamed myself," she says.

"Embarrassed, humiliated, inadequate, ashamed," adds Ernest. "We'd been taught that kids were a reflection of their parents, and in the evangelical home-schooling community it was hard, because when parents got together they compared families."

When it came to helping Emily, nothing seemed to work. They tried taking down the mirrors and hiding the scale. "I made high-calorie foods for her, but that just resulted in the rest of us gaining weight," says Yvonne.

Yvonne wishes she'd talked about it more with Ernest, believing that might have helped sustain her as well as Emily. She urges parents who feel helpless to pray for patience—"lots of patience"—because, while you can take your child to the doctor and monitor her weight, you cannot make her better.

"Choose your fights carefully," says Ernest. "Cut them some slack. In retrospect, I realize some of the things we were concerned about weren't so crucial. Dr. Dobson's expression for the teen years is 'Just get them through it.' And never stop showing them that you love them."

A Parent's Role

You feel as though you're going crazy. Your child appears to be dying, and you're being forced to stand on the sidelines and watch. *This is wrong*, you think. *I'm this person's parent. I brought her into the world. It is my responsibility to fix my child.*

Being a mother myself, I understand. It hurts me just to see my sons battling a cold. While there are steps I can take to ease their discomfort, I cannot mend the cold. I cannot create a cure. I can only hold them close, kiss their crusty noses, offer a tissue, and pray.

I realize a cold will not kill. But, in as much as it seems your child is dying, she has not yet hit rock bottom. As frustrating and as maddening as the reacting stage is, your child is still very much alive. So do not panic.

You will know when your child hits rock bottom; at that point, both you and your child will feel desperate. Currently, she is feeling strong, powerful, and almost happy, not realizing the full extent of the illness, not knowing it will one day kill her.

This stage is the addict's honeymoon. Your child is surfing the waves of adrenaline. That is why it's important to wait. Even as she loses weight, even as the fights escalate, it's important to wait.

Healing cannot be hurried. It must be wanted, not forced. Soon, the rush will pass and your child will get scared. Soon she will realize how very weak she is, and the addiction will become slavery. Your child will want to break free, but won't know how to live without it. It's this moment you are waiting for.

Choice Morsels

Pray, pray, pray

Even when the words stop, keep praying. Keep bowing and bending and being before the Lord. Read Psalms and bleed Psalms; let God hear your heart even through your silence, through your gasps for grace. You don't need to tell Him, for He already knows. You just need to come before Him and offer the sacrifice of the heart.

Don't fake it with God. He knows the truth. He knows that you're angry, scared and confused. He knows you feel riddled with guilt and shame. He knows your pillowcase is soaked with tears each morning. He wants to sit with you, hold you, and reassure you that He *is* sovereign, and nothing can change that.

And more than that, He is Father to your Child, and He hurts with you. He understands when you need to yell and scream and ask, *Why? Why is this happening to me?* And His answer will be one of mercy, for you are not to blame, and He knows this.

So let His whispered words soothe you in the silence of your prayers. And don't stop. Don't stop knocking on heaven's door, even as the persistent widow in the parable. Because prayer makes a way where there is no other.

Wait, don't Weight

Inasmuch as you pray, wait. Don't jump in with fix-it-all answers. Pick your battles wisely.

I understand the need to feel as though you're doing something. With that in mind, here are some tips for how to wait productively:

- **Remove all body-image temptations**, such as the weigh scale, fashion magazines, TV, and any unnecessary mirrors.
- **See a counselor** who has been through the eating disorder journey, preferably a counselor of the same gender and personality type as your son or daughter. Make it clear to your child that this person is not there to threaten them or force them to recover, but to listen.
- **Monitor your child's weight** by taking him for regular check-ups.
Keep your door open. Let your child know you are available to listen, and that you care.
- **Keep your mouth shut**. Refrain from making negative comments or judgments; just listen.

• **Continue to care for your other children**. Make an effort to spend one-on-one time with each of them. They, too, will be feeling helpless, and will be watching to see how you respond.

• **Read the Bible consistently**, morning, noon and night. Read it with your entire family at the supper table, for God convicts through His word. And read it in the hush of early morning, that you might derive strength for the day unfolding.

• **Find an outlet**, be it a friend who has gone through this before, or an art class, or an early morning jog. Make a way to stay moderately busy so you're not always thinking about ways you could be helping (when in fact, you simply need to pray and wait).

• **Love on your spouse**. Be close, as never before. Make moments for each other, and do not play the blame game. Each of you is hurting. Each of you is in love with your hate-filled child. Be a team of prayer, and find fellowship in one another's suffering.

Chapter 8
Friends' Perspective

Melissa's Story

THE SUN WAS HIGH in the young September sky. Melissa Bob served the birdie to Emily, her friend who'd just returned from a summer at her grandparents' farm. The friend she no longer recognized.

Emily's bony arm reached up to hit the birdie and she used both hands to swing the racket. Melissa returned it a couple more times and by that point, Emily was sweating and gasping.

"I'm so tired," she said and Melissa felt something heavy fall within her. Who was this girl who was all sharp edges and no strength? Emily had always been thin, but nothing like this sunken-cheek girl.

Yet she didn't say anything, not wanting to judge nor offend the quiet, sweet-voiced minister's daughter. And so, they went indoors and Melissa let Emily paint her nails.

The following day was Harvest Festival—an annual event at which vendors showed off their country wares, from steam equipment to old-time crockery, to youth's competitive jams and wood carvings.

Melissa and Emily had gone every year together, and this year was no exception, save for the stares people gave them when they arrived. The way parents pulled their kids close and hurried away as Emily approached.

Melissa scrunched fingers into fists, wanting to punch those who whispered and pointed. Yet at the same time, she didn't blame them.

Emily had become a skeleton.

A Friend's Role

What Now?

You've been friends for years. She has always been careful about what she eats, but you didn't notice anything particularly odd until now.

Your friend is no longer herself. She seems overly preoccupied with counting calories and spending time in the bathroom. Her face scares you; weight that should be there isn't, and you can see more than you ever wished to.

You're tempted to run away and hide, but you know that this person needs you now, more than ever. So what should you say? What should you do?

Meek and Mild

"The first time I saw her, I was in shock," Melissa recalls. "She left to see her grandma as 'Emily,' but came back someone I didn't recognize—a shadow of a person. I could see all of her bones and I didn't know what had happened to my friend, but I knew she was still in this body and she just needed help."

To process her thoughts, Melissa talked with her mom. "She told me to just be Emily's friend, and be there for her."

As hard as it was, Melissa made an effort not to mention the weight loss. "I just saw Emily and accepted her," says the forestry graduate. "I knew her family was going to help her. I just wanted to be her friend; to be there and support her. I didn't want Emily to think I was scared of her condition."

Nevertheless, some of Emily's other friends found they were unable to hide their fear when they saw her.

"She was so thin," recalls Marney Stewart, an elementary teacher on St. Joseph Island. "I remember feeling so afraid for her. Her face looked so different. I remember seeing wrinkles from where the skin was pulling over her cheekbones. Wrinkles where wrinkles should not have been on someone so young."

Marney tried to act casually, but didn't know how to talk to this gaunt stranger.

Sarah Bingham didn't know, either. "I didn't realize Emily was anorexic until I saw her at the festival," states the high-school English teacher. "I remember she looked like skin and bones. I could see the outline of her braces through her skin."

Both Sarah and Marney hugged Emily, feeling her ribs through her cotton shirt, and then walked away. But a few months later, after

Emily's parents admitted her into the hospital, Sarah and Marney helped to throw a pizza party for her in the hospital lounge.

Prior to the party, Melissa came to visit Emily. "I remember the nurse coming in and asking how many times she'd peed, and Emily answered her, a little embarrassed. I didn't know why she wouldn't ask Emily that stuff in private; it seemed a little mean to me. I also remember watching 'Fern Gully' with her in the hospital room."

Melissa didn't know if Emily wanted to get better. She just knew she missed being with her friends.

Blunt and Bold

"I tried to find a way around Emily not wanting to eat," says government employee and silversmith Jennifer Zidek. "I remember thinking she looked terrible...so, so very skinny, and pretty gross. Bones protruded from every part of her body...and it was ugly, but she thought it was pretty. People would stare at her when we went out. I didn't like it. She acted like she didn't want to change. Like it wasn't something she saw as a problem; like she enjoyed how grossly thin she was."

Jenny was loyal, as Melissa had been, but her tactics differed. While Melissa was meek and mild, Jenny acted boldly. Yet she always spoke the truth—in love.

"Sometimes I felt as though I got through, and Emily would see what I was seeing, and hear me," she says. "It seemed as though progress was being made...but then she'd just go back. So I started to get more aggressive and tried to make a bigger impact. I was determined to have her see what I saw."

Persistent love ever knocking at the door of a disordered eater's heart is what eventually gets through. You cannot shove the door open. Instead, keep knocking. And one day, your friend will hopefully open up and let you in.

"The one time we went out for a walk, many passing people stared...it was uncomfortable. That was when I thought this needed to be addressed in a more assertive way," Jenny admits. "I understand that my blunt words started to make a difference in how Emily was perceived, not only by me, but perhaps by others. I know the words

I said hurt, but it made a difference. I just think that no one was as willing to say the horrible reality about how it looked and what could happen to her if this continued."

Closer than a Brother

Yours is a unique role. Your eating disordered friend has selected you to be his friend, which is a rare gift. Disordered eaters shove most people away, keeping close only those they don't feel threatened by. So yours is a relationship to guard and respect.

As Melissa and Jennifer demonstrated, it's crucial to remain loyal to a friend during these black hours. As much as her sickness is hurting or confusing you, your friend needs you, even if it's just to be a silent comrade. After all, this illness stems from issues such as lack of control, low self-esteem, depression and loneliness—issues that will only worsen if the person is abandoned in his lowest moment.

That being said, it's very important that you find someone you can vent to, as Melissa did with her mom. You need an outlet, as much as your sick friend does. Someone to help you process what you're seeing. Someone who will pray with you, and give you the advice you're longing for.

Your loyalty will pay off. As Emily's condition worsened, she called Jenny on more than one occasion, secretly hoping to hear what no one else would tell her—*You need help.*

And due to Melissa's persistence and consideration, Emily opened up to her the afternoon she was painting Melissa's nails; the same afternoon she had no energy to play badminton; a few days before she was admitted into the hospital.

"Do you think something's wrong with me?" Emily asked.

Melissa swallowed, then said, "I *am* scared for you. You've lost a lot of weight."

That was all. But because Emily trusted Melissa, it was enough to make her believe something was indeed wrong—and perhaps she *did* need help.

If you stick closer than a brother, your sick friend will feel comfortable confiding in you when the rest of the world has turned its back. Don't feel as if you need to do anything with the information he has given you, unless your friend is planning to commit suicide (in which case, it's necessary to inform her parents or someone in authority *immediately*).

Otherwise, your supportive friendship—in which you admit to not liking what she's doing to herself—could be the one thing to convince your friend that she needs help.

Things *Not* to Say/Do

Insult. While your friend may be fearfully thin, looking much like a prisoner in a concentration camp, it's important to hold your tongue and speak uplifting words in her presence.

One of the reasons she is so sick is because of low self-esteem, so keep this in mind when you converse together, and attempt to be respectful of her feelings.

There's nothing wrong with admitting you're concerned about your friend. You can say something like, "You've lost a lot of weight, and I'm concerned about you," but say it with kindness, followed by, "I'm here to listen if you want to talk."

Any comment spoken as an insult will result in a defensive retort, and will ultimately sabotage your relationship.

Threaten. Eating disorders are very frustrating. It's so hard just to sit and watch your loved one hurt herself. It's a mental illness that requires time and patience; a sickness that depends on the Holy Spirit to soften the heart of the hurting. And healing will not be hastened by remarks such as, "Would you just eat already?!" or "I don't understand *why* you don't just eat!" or "You'd better stay out of the darn bathroom, or else!"

These are controlling words, not loving words. It is control which the disordered eater desires, so by threatening, you are attempting to rob that which he/she has tried so desperately to obtain. There is a lot of guilt attached to eating disorders, so lines such as these only perpetuate the belief that one is not good enough.

Inflict Guilt. Comments such as, "Why are you doing this to me?" or "Would you look at what you're doing to your boyfriend/family, etcetera?" are selfish statements, which will only drive your friend away.

As well, questions like, "Why are you doing this to yourself?" and "You have good things in your life; what's the problem?" will only drive a wedge between yourself and the friend you're trying to help.

Those with eating disorders are not intentionally trying to hurt others; rather, they're struggling, longing for an escape, and hoping someone might come alongside and offer them hope.

Statements like these will only increase their depression. Consider Jesus, who focused on helping sinners versus ridding them of their sin. Let's look at the person, and not the sickness.

Things *to* Say/Do

Be Supportive. When asked what advice she could offer to friends of disordered eaters, Melissa says, "Support them, and do not judge. Some people go through bumps in the road, and others go over mountains. But no matter the obstacle, you should hold their hand and help them."

Observe with Patience. "You can't force a person to accept that they need help," adds Sarah. "Be available and patient. Realize that, even if your friend decides to get help and get better, food issues will remain a struggle. Also, be observant. Your friend will be very good at hiding his or her struggles."

Tell the Truth. Jenny believes in stating the truth, so long as it is said in love. "You need to get through to them, so do and say whatever it takes (with support behind it, of course)."

Provide Perspective. She suggests encouraging a healthy alternative to the bad habits brewing. "Help them see how loved they are, and how this is hurting the ones they love. Show them that this is dangerous and the worst way to insult God, by treating oneself with such hatred."

Lastly, she says, "Don't give up on them. Ever."

Chapter 9

Professional Perspective

The Doctor's Diagnosis

FOLLOWING IS A LIST of suggested tips from Remuda Ranch for parents in the reacting stage.

Do's

- Know the signs of anorexia and bulimia.
- Learn what community and healthcare resources are available.
- Understand that eating disorders are complex. Recovery is not just a matter of will power.
- Discuss your concerns with the individual.
- Be compassionate; listen.
- Try to understand things from the person's perspective. Understand that persons with eating disorders often make decisions based on their feelings rather than on facts and logic.
- State what you have observed—list evidence of the problem.
- Express your concerns about the person's health and functioning, not just their weight.
- Indicate your conviction that the situation should at least be evaluated by a professional.
- Explain how you can help—with a referral, information, or emotional or financial support.
- End the conversation if it's going nowhere or if the person becomes upset. But if possible, leave the door open for further conversation.
- Have patience: If rejected, try again later, explaining that you are coming back because you think the situation is serious.
- Respond during emergencies: If the person is throwing up several times per day, passing out, complaining of chest pains, or talking about suicide, get help immediately.

- Find support for yourself. Talk to a counselor or healthcare professional; attend a support group for family and friends of those with eating disorders.

Don'ts

Several physical complications can be associated with anorexia nervosa, says Dr. Cabrera. Many of these problems are caused by behavior aimed at controlling Don't make promises you can't keep; i.e., Don't promise to keep the person's behavior a secret.

- Don't get over-involved. Know your limits. You are not a substitute for professional care.
- Don't oversimplify. Avoid platitudes like, "All you have to do is accept yourself as you are."
- Don't nag about eating or not eating, or spend time talking about food and weight.
- Don't be judgmental; don't say that what the person is doing is "sick," "stupid," or "self-destructive."
- Don't give advice about weight loss, exercise, or appearance.
- Don't say, "I know how you feel." You can demonstrate that you understand by paraphrasing what the person has said. •
Don't feel obliged to agree with the person's perspective or beliefs, even though you are making an effort to understand them.
- Don't bring a group of people to confront the person.

Hazards of Anorexia Nervosa

Several physical complications can be associated with anorexia nervosa, says Dr. Cabrera. Many of these problems are caused by behavior aimed at controlling body weight in an unhealthy manner, and most of these problems resolve once eating habits and weight have returned to normal. It is important for families to be aware of these complications should they manifest in one's child. (Keep in mind, not every anorexic will face these issues.)

Effects of binge-purge behavior

Injury to the esophagus (the tube connecting the mouth and stomach) can result from repeated vomiting. Acid and bile from the stomach irritates and inflames the membrane that lines the esophagus causing a condition known as esophagitis, which is sometimes severe enough to cause scarring and narrowing. This passageway may become so narrow that it is difficult for food to pass through. The physical stress of vomiting can cause tears in the lining of the esophagus. These tears may bleed massively or force the esophagus to rupture. This is a life-threatening condition that requires immediate surgery.

Injury to the stomach may occur due to binge eating. Frequent vomiting commonly causes gastritis, an inflammation of the stomach lining. Also, eating a large meal very rapidly, combined with slower emptying of food from the stomach, on very rare occasions, may cause the stomach to rupture, causing death from peritonitis.

Injury to the intestines, particularly the colon, commonly results from laxative abuse. Damage to the muscle and nerves causes loss of normal movement.

Lung complications occur when self-induced vomiting leads to aspiration of food particles, gastric acid, and bacteria from the stomach into the lungs, producing pneumonia.

Kidney and heart complications are often severe. Fasting, vomiting and other forms of purging result in a loss of fluid and crucial minerals from the body. Chronic dehydration and low potassium levels can lead to kidney stones and even kidney failure. Frequent vomiting leads to high alkali levels in the blood and body tissues. This may cause weakness, constipation and fatigue. Severe alkalosis and potassium deficiency can lead to an uneven heart rate or sudden death.

Injury to the skin occurs in various ways. Most over-the-counter laxatives contain phenolphthalein, which may cause sores in the skin and hyperpigmentation (brown or gray spots). Excessive and forceful vomiting may result in hemorrhages in the blood vessels in the eye.

Injury to the teeth is quite common. Chronic vomiting increases the acidity of the mouth and results in erosion of the teeth's enamel and dentin.

Methods of binge-purge

Laxatives may seem to move food through the body more rapidly and may relieve abdominal distention after binging, but they do not prevent the calories in the food from being absorbed. The temporary weight loss that is seen after using laxatives is mostly due to loss of water and minerals in the bowel movement, and will be naturally regained. Misuse of laxatives is harmful in several ways: they upset your body's mineral balance; they lead to dehydration; they damage the digestive tract lining; and they burn out your colon, so that you may experience severe constipation when you don't use them.

Diuretics, or water pills, increase urine excretion and can cause a sudden weight loss. A person who fails to distinguish between loss of body fat and loss of water may see this as a desirable effect and start using diuretics to lose weight. But because the only induced loss is water, the only gain is dehydration. In addition to causing dehydration, diuretics are dangerous because they can increase the loss of calcium, potassium, magnesium and zinc from the body. They can also cause rebound retention of salt and water, making your body more sensitive to diet changes.

Ipecac syrup, which is taken to induce vomiting, has been linked to deaths of several patients with eating disorders. Emetine, the active ingredient, can build up in tissue and cause muscle or heart weakness. Ipecac is toxic, whether taken as a single large dose or as a small dose that can build up over time.

Diet pills are often taken to help with weight loss. The best-known prescription pills are Dexedrine and Benzedrine, but over-the-counter drugs are also misused. These reduce appetite, but only temporarily. Typically the appetite returns to normal after a week or two, the lost weight is regained, and the user then has the problem of trying to get off the drug without gaining more weight. Warning: these drugs are of little use in achieving and maintaining weight loss and can become dangerously addicting and cause abnormal heart rhythms that can be fatal.

Fad diets promise rapid weight loss but actually encourage unhealthy dietary habits. They prey on the dieter's wish for quick results with little effort or make the diet seem exciting because the types of combinations of foods consumed are different from those normally eaten. People are attracted to such diets because of the dramatic weight loss (mostly water) brought about within a few days. Unfortunately, such quick weight-loss schemes do not help the body lose fat or provide the nutrients that are required to keep the body in optimal health.

The Counselor's Case

Mercy Ministries Canada Founder Helen Burns knows what it's like to be rendered helpless, having watched her own daughter, Danica, battle an eating disorder for 10 years.

When she first noticed her 13-year-old refusing to eat, "Anorexia wasn't even on my radar," says Burns. That was why she missed the 'recognizing' stage of her daughter's disorder, although looking back, she now recalls signs such as feigning sickness to skip meals, shoving food about her plate, speaking poorly about her body, doing excess exercise and 'eating' meals in her room.

"I began to pray and read about it," recalls Burns who, together with her husband, John, pastors Relate Church in the Greater Vancouver Area. "I prayed before approaching Danica because I felt my heart needed to settle; I didn't want to bombard her with my thoughts."

Then, one day, she asked Danica if she was starving herself. And Danica replied, "Yes, I am, and I'm really, really scared."

Not every disordered eater will recognize he/she has a problem, particularly in the midst of the disease, but "God had gotten a hold of her," says Burns.

Nevertheless, "She didn't understand the anorexia completely either, so I felt very, very helpless."

With little information at hand, Burns and her husband sought to create a support network comprised of pastors, doctors, counselors and friends. "We were just trying to get her to eat, and to stay on top of it, because we didn't know extensive long-term help was available," she says.

They learned later that the disease stemmed from much deeper issues—issues that included being the middle child, an abnormal focus on body image in spite of believing she was beautiful, and an inner voice that consistently told her she was a problem, a nuisance, who didn't deserve to live.

"She was definitely more out-spoken than the others, but she was never a problem," insists Burns. "Yet something was telling her she was."

Initially, Burns thought they could just keep praying and the problem would resolve itself, yet it took years of wading through the depths of the disease for Danica to emerge victorious.

Talk it Out

"We talked a lot," says Burns. "I had to stop trying to fix her, and I had to listen."

Instead of making the focus of each day whether or not Danica ate, "I needed to keep the door open to her as much as possible."

She warns against putting high expectations or demands on one's child, for that will push him/her away. "I had to say, 'No matter what, I'm here; you can count on me.'"

As a result, Danica felt she could talk to her mother about anything.

"Mom was safe," Burns says. "I was the one person she could go to."

Person versus Problem

Whether Danica had a good day or a bad one, "I had to stop being terrified in the sense of feeling rendered helpless; my terror only amplified everything."

Instead, Burns admitted to God she couldn't do this on her own. She put Danica's life in God's hands, and He gave her the strength to see past the problem to the person.

"I think, as parents, we get obsessed with the problem because it freaks us out, but I just had to keep listening to her heart and praying. I decided that whatever she did, it wouldn't make me love her any less."

Calm Down

Burns intentionally became the stabilizing factor in her child's life. "If I could believe (that God was healing and helping), then it was like she could believe for herself."

As a result, Danica's disease never reached dire straits. "We were always able to have a plan. We were always engaged in talking."

This is not to say they both didn't fly off the handle at each other, but there was always a plan of recovery in place.

Danger of Deception

In spite of Danica's willingness to recover, she became adept at deceiving, not only her parents, but herself, into thinking she was better.

"Anorexia became masterful; she knew how to fool us." This backwards slide would occur whenever Danica began to believe she was okay. Her guard would let down, and the disease would again take hold, in spite of her parents insisting, "You don't have to pretend you're doing well if you're not; we're not going anywhere."

As the years wore on, Danica's anorexia turned into bulimia in an attempt to heed the voice.

Write On

The cure presented itself through the pages of a journal.

"She would go get her journal and write down every thought, every horrible thought, filtering nothing, and she wouldn't let herself stop writing until she'd written the truth about her value, as seen through God's eyes."

And slowly, over time, the more Danica wrote, the more she began to differentiate between the voices in her head: the one being the enemy's, telling her she was useless and fat; the other, being God's, whispering extraordinary, gracious love.

"That's her miracle," Burns states. "She'd start in such a dark place, then practice the discipline of writing the truth; taking the time to write about her true value according to the Word of God, until there was a victory, a turning around of her focus."

To this day, Danica, now a mother of two girls, continues to journal in an attempt to recognize the truth.

Parent to Parent

Burns doesn't believe she would have been able to endure a decade of disease if it weren't for her support network.

"I had people around me who were open to knowing how the anorexia made *me* feel," she explains. This was crucial, she adds, as, being televised pastors, Burns and her husband are constantly being forced into a very public role. "We had amazing people around us whom we could talk to."

She encourages parents struggling in the reacting stage to surround themselves with caring individuals. "You need to have a place that feels safe, a way to vent. When you have a child with an eating disorder, it hugely affects the whole family. Parents need support."

Couple to Couple

Additionally, Burns says, it's important to nurture one's spouse. "John and I had to be protective of our marriage," she explains. "It's hard not to blame each other."

They had to make a conscious, daily decision to stay on the same page. "Anorexia does not want to just take out your child; it wants to destroy your marriage. We were on Team Danica. We were doing this together. We had to feel safe with that."

Again, finding a support network will not only provide accountability but encouragement during this long and arduous process. If possible, seek out couples who've already undergone the disease with their own son/daughter; couples whose hearts break with yours, couples who will dedicate days and nights to praying alongside you on behalf of your loved one.

Believer to God

When you're rendered helpless as a parent, says Burns, you tend to panic. Yet the Bible urges, if anyone lacks wisdom, ask of the Father.

"I lived desperately close to God, begging Him to help me,"

she admits. "I'd say, 'God, I don't know what to do or say today.' I felt like I was leaning so hard on Him."

With few books or resources to fall back on, God's wisdom was all Burns had. "I relied on the truth of the Word of God, and on Him speaking to me," she says. "He helped me understand; He helped me to love, no matter what, and to see Danica's heart; to not be moved by fear, but by faith."

There were moments in which God would tell Burns to take Danica for a drive or a walk, and moments in which He said, "Now is when you need to be Mom," and Burns would know she needed to speak firmly, yet in love. Always in love.

When your child doesn't want help, and you can't fix it, that's when prayer plays a part, says Burns. "It can go where you can't."

If you start to insist on doing things your way, "you push (your children) away, and cause them to hide more; then the process takes longer for them to come around." Instead, "We have to do everything we can to tear that wall down."

Chapter 10

Prayer

Dear Heavenly Father,
WE COME TO YOU as broken people. Broken, spent, and discouraged, we come, because we have nowhere else to go. We come and lay before You, begging for Your kindness in our time of need. We thank you, LORD, that "we have a great high priest who has passed through the heavens—Jesus the Son of God"—and we hold fast to that confession.

"For we do not have a high priest who is unable to sympathize with our weaknesses, but One who has been tested in every way as we are, yet is without sin. Therefore, we approach the throne of grace with boldness, so that we may receive mercy and find grace to help us at the proper time." (Hebrews 4:14-16)

We thank You, also, that You are all-knowing, all-empowering, and everywhere, present. We give thanks that You knew this moment before it ever came to be, and that You are in control. We praise You, God.

We hurt, LORD, for our loved one. We ache for ____, who is refusing to eat, and who is unintentionally destroying our family and our home.

We hurt, and we feel angry and betrayed, LORD. Where are You right now? Where are You when all we can hear is screaming? Where are You when ____ throws his/her plate against the wall? When we struggle to know what to say or do, and when the rest of the world judges us for not being better parents/siblings/friends?

Show us Your face in this pain-filled time. Draw close to us, as we draw close to You, and remember us. Remember our names, our needs, our hearts.

And teach us, LORD. Teach us patience and perseverance, so we might one day know character, and hope. (Romans 5:4) It is hope we're longing for, LORD. Give us a vision for what You want to do in this situation, a vision that will motivate us to love in the face of hate.

Speak to us Your truths and Your plans. Hold us in Your arms, giving us supernatural strength. And help us, LORD; send ministering angels to soothe our hearts as we strive to be understanding, gentle, and patient, when all we want to do is fix.

We trust You, LORD, to heal our loved one. To mend his/her hurts, in the deep-rooted places. We trust You, LORD, to bring health and new life where death is trying to reign. You are the Giver of life. You are the Great Healer. Nothing is beyond You.

Even now, when it seems like our child/sibling/friend is choosing to die, we believe You are re-creating. You are making a miracle. Increase our faith, LORD, for sometimes it's so hard to believe. Give us eyes to see beyond the obvious. Give us supernatural vision.

We come against the enemy and everything he wants to do in ____'s life; we come against him in Jesus' name and declare life and healing for our child/sibling/friend. No weapon formed against him/her shall prosper. (Isaiah 54:17)

We ask forgiveness, LORD, for the ways in which we've hurt You, and for the ways we've hurt our loved one. Let nothing we do or say stand in the way of ____'s recovery.

Amen.

Part III

RECOVERY

*How to help a disordered eater
who wants to get better*

Chapter 11

Child's Perspective

My Story

AFTER FOUR YEARS OF slow and steady starvation, I had finally quit eating altogether. No longer was I striving for a smaller size; I knew I was thin. Rather, I was trying to get rid of myself altogether.

Afraid of losing control and gaining weight, I had eaten less and less every day, until finally, I ate nothing. And every time I saw the lowered digits flashing red on the scale, a warm hand rubbed away the fear in my chest letting me "go" for just a little bit longer.

Laying there that autumn day in 1993, purple under the green sheet, I knew I'd done all I could. For some reason my body was refusing to let me lose any more pounds. And in some strange, sad way I felt relieved. My mission was complete. I was tired of fighting my family, my friends, and my Heavenly Father. I was exhausted from fighting fear.

In those quiet moments I gave in to the love that had spared my life, and decided to get better.

***

I had spent the summer at my grandparents' farm. Away from threats of Cod Liver Oil, my mum's constant watchful eye, the tearful begging, the menus, and the counseling, I cut down drastically on my eating.

It got so that I was eating a peach for breakfast, a few pickles for lunch, and a spoon of corn for supper. Afternoons were spent skipping rope or going for long walks.

I had never been thinner, and I marveled at the way my cheekbones jutted from my skin, at the way I could feel each of my ribs as I lay in bed at night.

Feeling for bones became a pastime, a twisted pleasure. Later, I would realize I hadn't truly seen what I looked like. I would look at photos from that time period and nearly vomit, seeing a skeleton;

whereas then, I'd seen a thin, beautiful girl in the mirror.

It wasn't until I returned home at the end of the summer that I began to wonder if things hadn't gone too far. I suddenly had no energy to run. While playing baseball in the park, I couldn't lift the bat. And people had started to hurry past me on the streets.

Then, my parents told me I wouldn't be returning to school that fall. Instead of entering grade eight, I'd be admitted into the general hospital in Sault Ste. Marie, Ontario, where I'd stay until I decided to get better.

At that point, I wept and stormed and promised to recover on my own—I would eat, I said, if only they'd let me enter grade eight. But the decision was final. My parents refused to budge, and so, in retaliation, for the next couple of days before entering the hospital, I didn't eat at all.

This was why, as I lay shivering from hypothermia on the hospital bed, I felt frustrated, for despite eating nothing, I'd been unable to drop any more weight. My body had called stalemate. My body was rebelling.

And secretly, I was relieved. My hair was falling out, my nails were cracking, and in spite of wearing a size one, my clothes were falling off. Worst of all, doctors were saying I wouldn't be able to have children.

On the way to the hospital, I'd seen a beautiful, muscular woman jogging, and in a moment, I had known: I wanted to get better. This was no way to live. This was hell.

Knowing I'd done all I could, and knowing I would die if I continued, I chose that day to live. I began to eat the moment nurses placed a tray full of food in front of me. And I couldn't believe how good the food tasted.

Over the next three months, as my weight slowly climbed, I was shocked that I didn't balloon outwards as I'd always thought I would. Even though I was gaining weight, I couldn't see it; I just felt stronger and happier.

My hair stopped falling out in clumps, my nails grew long, and I finally had the energy to concentrate on my schoolwork, completed via correspondence.

One night, friends from school came to the hospital and threw me a surprise pizza party. The next morning, the nurses weighed me and said I could go home. I was 80 pounds.

Once at home, I continued to gain weight. I was more than willing to keep following the dietician's menus so I might pursue this new life that was boys and friends and parties; this life that wasn't consumed with counting calories or planning out the next day's meals, or trying to die.

Resurfacing

For a decade, my disease lay dormant. From the ages of 13 to 23, I thought I was better, watching people whom I deemed "beautiful" as they dished up at potlucks or family functions, mimicking their actions like a mindless puppet. I was a copycat infant when it came to food.

At the same time, I nursed at the breast of God, who reminded me daily of my identity in Christ.

Those were happy years, filled with mission trips, boys and a restored relationship with my family. And, at the age of 16, I got my menstrual cycle. There was a chance I could still have children.

Then, like a clap of thunder on a sunny day, the illness reappeared, awakened by a seemingly innocent comment.

"You've gained a bit of weight." It was that one remark from an unaware observer which regurgitated three more years of the same battle. Only this time, this newly married girl knew what she was doing.

I'd been through the routine before, and realized what I was risking: A wonderful, godly husband who loved me more than life itself; any hope of ever having children; a ministry to teenage girls who looked up to me, and most importantly, a maturing and fruitful relationship with God.

The heart of the problem was twofold. When recovering from my initial struggle with anorexia, I had failed to train myself in nutrition. I'd failed to get to know my body, to educate myself, to find a healthy lifestyle that suited my body type. Instead I'd settled for mimicking those around me—which, ironically, was what got me into trouble in the first place. I hadn't learned to eat for myself.

Additionally, I'd ignored the issues—such as bitterness towards my family, low self-esteem, need for control, and perfectionism—which had instigated the anorexia in the first place. So, with the slightest tremor, the flimsy scaffolding I'd tacked together fell apart.

There came a point in spring of 2006—a very dark and deathly point—which defined my destiny. It happened on the streets of Alberta. There, during an ear-splitting fight with my husband over food, I tried to drive the car into oncoming traffic.

Our relationship had been strained by hurt feelings and power trips. Food was the underlying issue. Involved in ministry all day long, we saved up our tiredness and worries to dump on each other at night.

I exercised every morning, skipped breakfast and lunch and drank 10 cups of coffee a day. I became an insomniac, unable to sleep for a year and a half.

On that breezy spring day in the middle of the Albertan highway, my husband gave me a choice: It was either him or food. He couldn't do it any longer.

Chapter 12
Spouse's Perspective

Trent's Story

SHE WORE HIPPY-CLOTHES AND blue-beaded necklaces. Her long blond hair swung as she danced long and laughed out loud. He thought, *I have to know her... This girl who seems so free.*

She told him, later, of her past. She told him as they lay on the living room floor listening to Bon Jovi and twirling fingers tight. She shared of years long ago, spent starving herself. He nodded once, and that was all. She ate now, and that was what mattered.

And when he lay sick in bed and asked her to marry him, he felt her cool hand on his forehead as she nodded and squealed yes.

He had no idea that this wild girl who wanted babies would soon turn into a different person. A person who no longer wanted to eat. A person who no longer wanted children.

Recognizing

"I first noticed she had a problem when I made popcorn," Trent, a math and science high school teacher, recalls. "I always added butter to the popcorn. She refused to eat it, and got very upset at me and popped another bag for herself. I thought, *It's just a bit of butter....*"

It was their first year of marriage, and Trent couldn't understand what had happened to his carefree wife. "I don't think it is something anyone else can understand. I think it's spiritual mostly. I don't think you can rationalize why someone struggles with it, because they're starving their body by choice, and that's not something you can, should, or want to understand—understanding it justifies it, and I couldn't do that."

Reacting

The decline was slow but steady. Being at work, Trent didn't see the girl who'd stopped eating breakfast and started skipping lunch; he only saw the girl who ate pizza voraciously with him at supper.

But then Emily stopped being able to sleep. "The insomnia really affected both of us," he says. "Emily would cry in bed, and, having read that insomnia was a sign of anorexia, I mentioned that to her. She blew up at me."

Emily began sleeping on the couch, catching four hours before rising to exercise. She would drink multiple cups of coffee while at work, eating nothing until supper.

"I wanted to help her," Trent says, "but there wasn't anything I could do besides pray because it was a decision she had to make. The quality of our lives was going downhill, but she had to see that."

One day in autumn, in their third year of marriage, Trent and Emily attended a family luncheon at his Grandma's farm. Trent was worried, knowing she never ate lunch.

As Emily proceeded to dish up her plate, he whispered, "I'm so proud of you." She shot him a dirty look. "This is my one meal for the day," she hissed. His heart sank hard.

"Anorexia is an extremely superficial, selfish disease," Trent says. "The third world suffers anorexic symptoms, not because they have the disease but because they can't afford to eat. They die, longing for food. And yet there are girls dying because they've rejected food."

Everything changed, six months after the family luncheon, on a trip home from Calgary to Edmonton. In spite of spending a weekend with friends; in spite of spring sunshine and games of bocce and a trip to the zoo, Trent and Emily were fighting. She had eaten nothing that day, as per usual, and was so angry she tried to drive the car into traffic.

"I decided I'd had enough, because Emily was going down a road, so to speak, without me," says Trent. "She was letting anorexia make the decisions."

It had been three years. Three years of not sleeping. Three years of not eating. Trent was finished. And so, he gave his wife an ultimatum: it was him, or food. She had to choose.

Recovery

Emily chose Trent.

"Right away she started trying to eat," Trent recalls. She met with a mutual friend and discussed what to have for meals, then began eating three times a day. The meals started off small—a hard-boiled egg with a glass of orange juice for breakfast, a salad for lunch—but slowly, over time, Emily gained the courage to eat more.

Then, they left for Korea. Emily quit her job at a nonprofit Christian newspaper, and Trent gave up his position as staff with Young Life. Together, they made new beginnings in a foreign land.

As Emily learned to trust her body and eat when she was hungry; as she stopped worrying about weight and began to enjoy food (and life) again, sleep came more easily.

And eventually, over time, after Trent and Emily moved back to Canada and bought a little house in Ontario, she began to want kids again, too.

Choosing to Live

By Grace Alone

Years of starvation had not only destroyed my body, they had ravaged my mind, so I no longer knew what was best for myself. When I looked in the mirror, I saw a beautiful girl. Others shrunk away in horror at the sight of a skeleton.

Being a mental disease, eating disorders rob one of the energy needed to choose good over evil. Satan takes advantage of this vulnerable state, and blinds, deafens and confuses the disordered eater into thinking he/she is fighting a noble war. Only prayers can fix this twisted reality; only the grace of God can leak into one's mind and heal.

Dying to Oneself

Once grace intervened on my deathbed, and I was willing to recover, I did—but only with the help of others. I was like a newborn, learning how to eat, think and breathe all over again through the eyes of God. Anorexia had been my identity; without it, I felt empty.

One day, I walked down the country road in front of my house, asking God who I was apart from my eating disorder. As I stood on a hill overlooking a tangle of snowy trees, I decided that, until I knew who I was, I would merely act as Jesus did, trusting that, as I did, my true personality would eventually shine through.

This need to let go of one's disordered identity is why many do not fully recover. It's also why I relapsed. I hadn't wanted to fully let go of my ability to choose anorexia. I'd become attached to my ED and didn't know who I was without it. I wanted the best of both worlds—to stay in control of my eating, but be healthy enough to fool everyone (including myself) into thinking I was no longer sick.

Full Recovery

Because eating disorders are an illness of the mind, once a person decides to get better, he/she will, for the most part. Yet, only 30 to 40 percent *fully* recovers, statistics tell us. And, depending on how acute the illness, the disordered eater will most likely need some form of aid in order to mount the seemingly insurmountable.

Even though it took a relapse for me to fully recover, I eventually realized that health is not determined by size. Rather, it coincides with a frame of mind.

Disordered eating stems from seeing oneself through the eyes of the mirror; healthy eating, through the eyes of Christ. To eat healthily means to eat until one is full, versus consuming an allotted amount of something. Eating healthily means honoring one's body; listening to one's physical cues, learning when one is hungry, knowing what the body needs—be it protein, carbohydrates, fats, or fruits and vegetables—and eating accordingly.

Anorexia and Alcoholism

While it may be cliché, in the same manner as a recovering alcoholic, a recovering disordered eater needs to resist certain temptations. These include the scale (which should be removed entirely or hidden from sight), calorie charts on grocery packages, fashion magazines, television shows such as *America's Next Top Model* which draw attention to the body, and anyone who might make your loved one question his/her decision to recover.

Alcoholics Anonymous also encourages recovering addicts to fall on their faith, receiving a spiritual "high" versus a drunken one. Disordered eaters should do the same. Not eating is a form of "high;" an addictive kick that is hard to live without.

Allowing oneself to fall in love with God is crucial to recovery. Reading and memorizing uplifting passages of scripture, attending Christian conferences, and singing praise songs will help to reshape one's thinking and make one hungry, both for food and for the presence of God.

Personally Speaking

Choosing to recover is, for most disordered eaters—anorexics in particular—making the choice between life and death.

For me, daily life had become a slow form of dying. I realized I didn't want to die when God intervened through the image of a woman running. As is the case with many anorexics, I found meaning in beauty. The woman running outside my window portrayed life as vibrant and lovely, and I wanted that. I wanted to live abundantly, fully, and free.

And, with that simple realization, it was as though cotton fell from my ears, and my parents' words finally made sense: "Food is like gas for a car," they had said. "A car can't run without it."

I could no longer run. I could barely walk, or hold a bat. And thanks to my parents' discerning intervention, I could no longer attend school, which had become, for me, a means of escape. My parents knew this, and wisely removed it in a desperate attempt to save my life. I could no longer pretend things were okay.

I had been starving myself for four years. In addition to food, I'd denied myself anything that had made me feel good: my mother's hugs, laughter, and any kind of relaxation. I'd put my body through rigid self-denial, and after four years, I was ready to give in to love, or die.

After all, extreme self-denial is a form of self-hatred. And hatred is exhausting.

Following my relapse at the age of 26, God intervened a second time. He showed me grace. He understood my fall back into anorexia was not a deliberate attempt to sin, but rather, a desperate attempt to maintain control of my independence in spite of getting married.

He knew the disease had become master, and so used my husband to give me an ultimatum. And that ultimatum came at the perfect time—when I wanted to either die (as exhibited by me trying to drive into traffic) or get better.

God is always in control. Even when life seems not to be.

Chapter 13

Parents' Perspective

Ernest's Story

HE SAT ACROSS FROM Emily at Ann's Café, watched her pick apart the cinnamon bun then eat it, doughy flake by doughy flake. He cleared his throat and looked down at his nails, black from working on the van.

There was still so much to do, so many parishioners to visit—but that could wait. He was learning to stop and listen. He was learning to date his daughters.

"So how is school going?" Ernest said. "Was the transition pretty easy?"

Emily nodded. "Everyone's been very kind. Apparently I did more work than I needed to in the hospital. So, it's been good."

Every piece of bun was a victory; every sentence shared in love, a step closer to the healing she seemed to want. Ernest was scared to believe it, but, after four years, it was finally happening. His daughter was recovering from anorexia.

***

Emily had decided to get better, and her parents' relationship was on the mend. Over the years, they'd learned when to insist, and when to let go. They'd learned that life was more than a game of tug and war, and they'd started to become vulnerable in front of their children.

Ernest was taking his daughters on "dates" and playing baseball with his son; Yvonne had relaxed about the orange juice, and was spending less time in her flower beds and more time with her children.

"I was relieved when Emily 'chose' to recover, though wary that she could just as easily 'choose' anorexic patterns again when the mood hit her," admits Ernest, now the pastor of Living Water Christian Fellowship in Blyth, Ontario. "At least the forced weight gain at the hospital seemed to break the imprisonment in which weeks of hunger had ensnared her mind."

As days lengthened into years, and Emily's health returned, she began spending more time in the living room and less time in her bedroom. She began to laugh again, to hug her mum, and to ask her dad for help with homework.

"It was wonderful to have her responding more meekly and reasonably again," says Ernest. Nevertheless, he was still nervous around Emily, unsure whether this person was here to stay, or if the other would soon rear its terrifying head.

"I approached Emily tentatively, not wanting to risk a recurrence of previous flare-ups," he says. "I figured she was open to receiving help (on her terms) only because she was tired of the alternative consequences."

Life continued to have its jagged moments; fights still erupted, and tempers still rose. But efforts were being made. Yvonne took special care to cook healthy meals. She let her kids dish up their own plates. And she allowed Emily to make her own school lunches, again, exhibiting extreme trust.

With food in her stomach and meat on her bones, Emily was less prone to rage, and more open to reason. Yet she was focused on the future, not wanting to remember the past. It would take years, therefore, before she realized the damage done. Years before Emily felt any form of remorse for the way she'd destroyed her home. And years before she'd think to ask for forgiveness.

But even in the worst of moments—even when Emily screamed "I hate you," and mocked him in front of the family—Ernest forgave her. "I don't recall any ongoing 'grudge' or bitterness," says Ernest, "just a longing for her to be well again and able to enjoy life normally like the other three children."

When asked for his advice to other parents walking with their child on the road to recovery, Ernest states: "Pray lots; trust God; keep close to your spouse and other personal supports (friends, community, etc.); get help rather than trying to fight it on your own; keep loving them unconditionally, even when they blow up; be consistent; be honest with the other kids about what's going on, and don't sweat the small stuff."

Weighing in the Factors

Besides prayer and eventually forcing one's child into the hospital, there's not much one can do until the disordered eater chooses to get better. Because it's a mental illness, hinging on issues of control and perfectionism, healing requires the supernatural hand of God at work in the fragile state of a disordered eater's mind.

It can be hard, waiting for that moment; wondering if it will ever arise. And in the meantime, you think, Should I be admitting my child to the hospital? Should I be grounding her until she eats? And once your child decides to recover, do you let her do it on her own and trust her judgment? Or do you still depend on dietitians and the aid of hospitals?

There are three possible outcomes for a disordered eater—outcomes you must be aware of, difficult as they may be.

Firstly, your child may choose healing, perhaps months, or, as in my case, four years after the inception of the disease.

Secondly, he or she may decide to live with a mild form of the illness for the rest of his/her life.

And thirdly, as is the case with 10 to 20 percent of anorexics, he or she may die from related health issues within 10 years of contracting the illness.

A Parent's Role

How to help your child achieve full recovery

Some say an eating disorder is a plight one has to live with for the rest of one's life. And in certain cases, it may very well be a "thorn" in one's flesh such as Paul speaks of in 2 Corinthians 12. But this should not be assumed.

God rebuilds minds. He delights in making whole what once was broken. "Be transformed by the renewal of your mind," He urges in Romans 12:2. If this were not possible, would He ask us to do it?

This, then, is what we must pray and work towards, and believe in. For, "If you believe, you will receive whatever you ask for in prayer." (Matthew 21:22)

What to Do

Perhaps your child has just emerged from a treatment program. He/she is intent on getting better, and has made significant process. You're wondering, *What now?*

Coming home can take its toll on a newly recovered disordered eater. Because of this, it's important to make the transition as smooth as possible.

Keep in mind the parable of the prodigal son, who, upon arriving home, was treated to the finest of robes, the choicest of calves, the rarest of love. And his older brother became jealous, wondering, why not him?

The prodigal son's father responded, "My son, you are here with me always; everything I have is yours. But now we must celebrate and rejoice, because your brother was dead and has come to life again; he was lost and has been found." (Luke 15:31)

Don't be afraid to celebrate, to let your child know how grateful you are that he/she has made this choice, and how proud you are of him/her. Continue to celebrate as the days pass; become reacquainted with this newly revived daughter or son, and express love, acceptance and joy. For this is grace. And your child needs all the grace you can give as he/she learns to eat again.

At the same time, your child needs guidance. No doubt you've spoken with a dietitian and received sample menus; don't be afraid to go over them with your child and ask how you might make them more appealing. Involve her. Give her options. Ask what kinds of snacks she prefers. And take your child grocery shopping, slowly reintroducing her to the joy of food.

Above all, support your child's choices, and believe in her. She will sense this, and want to live up to it. Be gentle and kind, for your young one has been through a heavy bruising. Healing takes time and patience. Not every day will be a good one, but so long as there are more good days than bad, you can be encouraged.

Make food a non-issue. Count every mouthful a victory. And unless your child's weight starts to drop again, say nothing about the mouthfuls not taken.

Keep in mind, your child is a newborn when it comes to knowing the proper amount to eat, as well as how to think, act and speak without the influence of an eating disorder. Your child is redefining her personality. This is a difficult process, much like metamorphosis. One doesn't interrupt this kind of thing. One merely acknowledges, and prayerfully encourages.

Your child may make decisions you don't agree with; she may eat less than you'd like one day, but don't worry. This doesn't necessarily indicate a relapse. It might mean she was having a hard day, or perhaps she was just not hungry.

Even if you don't believe this, practice saying it to yourself, for with God, anything—including full recovery—is possible.

What Not to Do

Do not neglect your other children. Warn them, prior to their sibling's homecoming, that there will be a celebration. But don't forget about them.

It will take special strength to invest in each son and daughter during this time, but it's important. After all, everyone is nervous, wondering, *Will this work?* Afraid to hope for the years of disappointment.

Do not add to this apprehension; focus instead on making the transition smooth for everyone, and pray for wisdom in knowing how to do this.

Do not overdo it. Food has been an issue for years. Now is the time to relax and trust. By exhibiting trust, your once sickly child will slowly blossom.

Try not to talk about food unless he/she is refusing to follow the menu. Keep topics weight-free, and urge your children to do the same.

In the same vein, do not remark on how your recovering child is doing. Comments like, "You're looking healthy," or "It's nice you're not so bony anymore," could trigger a relapse.

I *cannot* stress this enough: eliminate any reference to size or weight from your vocabulary. While it's important to be encouraging, focus instead on your child's inward beauty.

Healthy Distractions

It may seem irreverent to think of God as a distraction, but I encourage families of disordered eaters to occupy their minds and hearts with scripture or worship music.

It's also important for a recovering disordered eater to pursue her talents. Many ED individuals—especially anorexics—are creative, sensitive souls. Perhaps your child is a musician; perhaps she loves paper-mâché, writing stories, or acting. In my case, I began writing stories and sketching furiously. I loved to sit in a mall and study people's faces as they walked by, then return home to draw.

This artistic outlet allows for those who once found their identity in food to form new identities. (I would dissuade more active outlets such as dance or cycling until exercise can be properly moderated and understood apart from the ED.)

What does God desire? "Faith expressed in love." (Galatians 5:6) When we have love, we have no need to fear. Christ loved humanity before time began—before the first calories were counted or the first mirrors reflected our vanity.

So rather than striving for the perfect size, encourage your loved one to hunger for perfect love, as expressed through creativity. Then, life will no longer be viewed from behind a thin veil. With time, she will see herself for who she truly is: A beautiful child of God.

Slowly but Surely

As with any mental disease, it may take years for a former disordered eater to learn to think for herself again. But don't be discouraged. Hard days will come and go. Some days will be more victorious than others. The important thing to remember is this: your child has chosen life. And that is something to celebrate, indeed.

Chapter 14

Siblings' Perspective

Keith's Story

HE HID BEHIND THE hospital door, listening. Down the hall, teens were pulling out their hair and muttering. Some sat quietly, while others looked at him with empty eyes. A girl who seemed just a shell of a being walked past counting her fingers and Keith thought of his 11-year-old sister behind the door and begged God to bring her home so they could be a normal family again.

They'd driven to Toronto five days ago and had spent the past four days visiting Canada's Wonderland, attending a Blue Jays' game and climbing the CN Tower. But the entire time they'd been thinking about the one who wasn't with them, the sibling locked behind closed doors in the psych ward of SickKids.

Keith was sure there had to be a better way than forcing food down a person's throat, but Mum and Dad were desperate. Emily had been sick for two years, now, and they were at their wits' end. So they'd come here.

Keith didn't know why he'd bought her the mug at the gift store. He wished he'd had the strength to smash it against the floor, shattering porcelain into countless angry pieces, fragmented like his family had become.

But he'd seen her face as they'd walked away, leaving her alone in that white-walled hospital room. He'd seen the way she'd huddled on the bed in her green hospital gown, the way she'd turned towards the wall, spinal cord sticking sharp through the gown, and he'd remembered, the girl she used to be.

The girl who had been his best friend. The one who'd made sand patties with him and cardboard costumes and had sat with him in buckets of water in Congo. She was hurting. And he missed her. So, he'd bought her the mug. The mug with the bear on it. The mug that said, "I love you beary, beary much."

He listened now, from behind the door, as Mum handed it to her. Listened as Emily tore off the paper and took the mug from its box. Then he shoved nine-year-old hands into his pockets as she screamed, "I don't need your stupid gifts!"

And he backed away slowly, wishing, oh wishing, he'd smashed it hard against the ground, seeing everything now through a wash of tears and feeling people's eyes on him, strange people's eyes in a strange hospital and he felt angry now, so very angry and betrayed, for he'd let down his guard and he had gotten hurt.

He ran a shaky hand under his nose, wiped it on his jeans. He'd spent his allowance on that mug. Now, Mum was explaining to Emily, telling her that he was standing outside the door, and Emily was gasping, saying, "Oh no, oh no," and she was coming to the door, her cheeks wet from crying and for a moment he knew. She was so, so sorry.

But then, he remembered the screaming, and he just looked at her with eyes that asked *Why?* And she shook her head, saying, "I love it, Keith, really. It's so amazing. Thank you," even as he walked away.

***

Emily didn't recover that week. In fact, she ate just enough to get out, and then, once at home, cut back even more. The anorexia lasted another two years. The mug had failed to do the trick. As a result, Keith resorted again to anger. And instead of wishing he could help her, he wished she would help herself.

Little did he know, that's what it would take: Emily choosing to help herself.

And in 1993, Emily decided to get better, when her parents admitted her into the general hospital.

"I'm not sure I trusted that she was serious about it, or that she would be serious about it for an extended period of time," Keith states.

Nevertheless, as time passed by and life slowly returned to normal, he and his sisters began to notice a difference in Emily.

"I remember when she was in grade 12, she spent more time upstairs, and opened up to us more," Meredith says. "I can picture her sitting on the living room floor, sketching a picture which compared different facets of life (one side was black and white, and the other was color). She seemed more relaxed and serious about her faith. Her sense of humor came out more, and there was less arguing."

"I figured that Emily had been able to realize that life was worth living," states Allison. "I felt like she was finally able to hear God's voice and not just the lies and angry thoughts that had been bumbling around in her head beforehand, and that she was willing to forgive all of us, and to move on."

Keith and Emily began to banter with each other at mealtimes, playing off each other's jokes and making light of situations. And slowly, their friendship was restored.

Nevertheless, they were all left wondering what had just happened. "Our family dealt with the anorexia much like we dealt with Nanny's death (our grandmother who committed suicide), by remaining silent and not discussing it," says Meredith. "That left me with a lot of questions that weren't answered until Emily shared her testimony (at camp), and I learned a lot more about what she'd been going through and the reasons she'd done what she had."

A Sibling's Role

Your sister or brother has decided to get better. For you, the sibling, this conjures up a number of feelings. Perhaps you're battling doubt; will he/she ever truly recover? Perhaps you're angry, feeling you can never trust him/her again, wondering what makes this particular time different from all the rest. Maybe you're feeling protective of your parents, or your other siblings, not wanting to see them get hurt, wishing your eating-disordered sibling would leave and never return.

Perhaps you've been disappointed one too many times, and you wonder if you can ever love your sibling again. Or maybe you're battling jealousy, afraid that now he/she has decided to get better, your parents will focus even more on him/her and leave you completely in the dark.

Sage Advice

"It's not your responsibility to change your sibling's eating patterns," says Meredith. "Simply be there for them. Be a friend, not a parent. Seek help for yourself when you are hurting. Your parents' attention may be focused on your sibling's obvious issues, but it's important that your less obvious needs are met as well.

"Find ways to communicate openly with your parents about how you feel and what you need, especially if you are feeling neglected. This will help you avoid falling into the same pit that your sibling did in order to get the attention you crave and need. If your parents aren't able to be there for you, find another caring adult who will be a good influence in your life."

"Be faithful and patient," Keith adds. "Love and support those in your family that accept your love, and be there for those that don't."

"And don't let yourself get trapped by focusing on all that seems to be going wrong, or on the problems your sibling and family are facing," says Allison. "Try to be thankful for every effort your sibling(s) and parent(s) make in showing love, whether to each other or to you personally. Encourage, even when you feel alone. Love whenever you're tempted to give in to defeat. Give time and space to those who need it, and mention kind words or thanks whenever possible.

"Just keep thanking God for whatever you can think of, and look forward to the future, knowing that He is good and He is faithful to you, to your family, and till the end of time. Don't give up, for 'He loves to prove himself faithful and more than enough to satisfy our hungry souls.'" (*Captivating*, Thomas Nelson, 2005, p. 141)

Choice Morsels

Following are some examples of how to walk in recovery alongside your sibling.

Faithfully Forgive

Forgive your sibling on a daily basis. Understand she never intended to hurt you. While it *was* her fault, she did not mean for things to get this bad, and has no doubt wanted help for a long time.

You have been wounded by your loved one, yes, but she has also been wounded. Be the bigger person, and approach your sister (or brother) with the words, "I love you. I'm sorry for whatever I've done in the past to hurt you. I forgive you for the ways you've hurt me. I'm so proud of you for the choice you're making right now to get better. Please let me know how I can help you."

It will not be easy. But God will reward you for taking this step, and He will give you the strength to keep forgiving your sibling, even if it's hour by hour. God tells us in the Bible to forgive 70 times seven times. (Matthew 18:22)

In other words, no matter how many times someone messes up, you are meant to forgive. Plain and simple. But you cannot do it on your own. God will give you the strength to forgive. Remember, forgiveness isn't a feeling. It's a choice. The feeling (of peace) *will* follow, but not necessarily right away.

Curb Your Words

The journey towards healing is not an easy one. For you, eating is most likely a simple ordeal—lifting utensil to mouth, chewing, swallowing, repeating until full. For your sibling, it is as complicated as engaging in battle. With every meal, she is entering a war-zone: the good news is, she is now fighting for the right side (life), but still dodging bullets intended to kill.

Your sibling needs your support in this fight. Your words can be used either for or against her. Learn to speak life-giving words. Learn to praise, without focusing on food, weight or calories. Look for ways to uplift your sibling. Recognize her gifts, and encourage them. Notice when she does her hair differently. And slowly, you will find mealtimes getting easier.

Resist the Urge

As aforementioned, this journey will not be easy. Some days will be good; others, bad. But resist the urge to generalize based on a single day. Don't assume your sibling is slipping backwards just because of a few lousy meals. Everyone is entitled to a bad day here and there.

So keep your chin up, because the stronger you are, the stronger everyone around you will be.

Seek Solace

You are not alone. Your siblings and your parents are on your team. Whenever you crave comfort or encouragement, or the strength to forgive, pray with one of your brothers or sisters, or ask your parents for some one-on-one time. If your parents are not available, do as Meredith suggests and seek a mentor who might motivate, challenge and uplift you. Join in the community around you, knowing they love you and want what's best for you.

Be Honest

Don't be afraid to talk to your sibling. Tell her how much she hurt you, and confess that you want to forgive, but are still holding on to some grudges. Ask her to pray for you, and share your doubts (i.e., that you're afraid she isn't serious about getting better).

But do it all in love. Do not accuse, threaten or insult. Recognize that, while it's healthy to keep the lines of communication open, your sibling is still hurting, and still very vulnerable to the disease. Be gentle, therefore, in your approach.

Take a Break

While you need to remain unified with your family, and to seek healing together (for all of you have been bruised and battered over the course of this disease), it's also crucial to take a break from each other.

Enjoy your friendships. Take time to have conversations, go on bike rides, go for runs, get a coffee, see a movie, do normal kid things which don't deal with matters so heavy (or light!) as eating disorders.

The more balanced you are, the calmer you'll feel. You won't resent your sibling for stealing so much attention, and you'll view the world through fresh eyes.

It's important to take care of yourself, to love yourself, so you might be of some use to your family.

Find an Outlet to Plug Into

As your sibling recovers, it's wise for you to find a way to vent your frustrations, thoughts, and emotions, either through sports, journaling, music, painting, or dance.

Release any tension and free yourself of negativity. Use this creative time to channel your heart towards God, and focus on spending time in His presence. And He will fill you with the love, hope and peace you're seeking.

Chapter 15

Professional Perspective

The Doctor's Diagnosis

RON BROUGHTON, M. Ed, LPC, has observed countless disordered eaters enter into the final stages of the disease. In general, says Broughton, eating disorders are resolved in one of three ways:

> 1. Primarily, and most often, the individual chooses to recover after hitting rock bottom.
> 2. Secondly, some acknowledge they have an illness prior to hitting bottom, and then choose to seek help.
> 3. Thirdly, there are those who never acknowledge the sickness and die without ever desiring recovery.

The latter, adds Broughton, is rare. The most common case is for a disordered eater to wake up near-death, and desperately desire life. "They then begin to make some improvement as they recapture life's goals and visions."

It is almost impossible, says Broughton, to help someone who doesn't want to be helped. The patient's life may be sustained for a period of time through force—feeding tubes, purge precautions (monitoring an individual who struggles to keep food down), etcetera—but without a will, there is no way.

"Professionals need to be persistent and let the patient know their behavior is only provided as a protection against the disease," he says. "It truly is not about us controlling the individual, although many patients think that is what we are doing."

Trust Factor

Prior to treating an individual, Broughton works at establishing a level of trust. This can take months.

"Difficult cases are slow to develop trust as they do not want to let go of the familiar thoughts, feelings and behaviors associated with the disease," he says. "However, we continue to work toward affirmation and confrontation of the disease in order to assist the individual in seeing what they struggle to see—that is, their imminent death."

It's risky to establish such a trust factor, for, having become accustomed to lying, disordered eaters cannot, in truth, be trusted. "When we relax controls on the patient by trusting them, they can take advantage of that and re-engage in the disease behavior," says Broughton, "thereby losing all ground gained in a short amount of time."

With this in mind, Brookhaven's approach has been to gradually release the controls that protect the patient from the disease. For example, purge precautions—interventions for those suffering from bulimia—are ordinarily 45 to 90 minutes, depending on the patient's ability to keep food down.

As the patient progresses, precaution time is decreased in order to deepen the trust. However, "Sometimes we have to increase the total time, as the person attempts to manipulate the time and other factors related to the precautions."

Treatment

Brookhaven Memorial Hospital is one of many treatment centers designed to help rock-bottom patients reach their goal of recovery.

Treatment differs per individual, Broughton says, as eating disorders are comprised of many facets, including "Control; identity issues; addictions; obsessive-compulsiveness; issues related to the adult maturation of the individual; severe cases appearing as delusional; attachment issues; factors related to various forms of abuse; borderline personality disorder or histrionic personality; brain injury due to malnutrition; anger problems related to control; family issues (attitudes, compositions and relationships) and last but not least, the genetic component (addressed earlier by Dr. Dena Cabrera)."

In order to decipher which of these issues are prevalent in an individual, Broughton treats each patient as separate from his/her disease. "I don't like it when the individual or the treating professional says, '*My* or *your* eating disorder,'" he explains, "or refers to the disease as 'ED,' like a friend. This implies that the individual is the disease, when they are not."

This loss of individual identity poses the greatest threat to recovery. "Many people I have worked with, in essence, become the disease," says Broughton. "Their whole life is consumed by the disease, the rituals and the manipulation; as such, who they are is the disease—they no longer have an individual identity."

During treatment, Broughton attempts to convince the individual that he/she is separate from the ED. He then works towards therapeutically confronting the individual's disordered behavior—the lying, manipulating, denial, and other components of the disease. "I balance confrontation with positive affirmation of the individual's abilities to defeat the disease, and affirmation of the individual's potential," he says. "I move towards a positive future, not the negative of the past."

This, he states, is a very long process. He urges therapists to remain focused, and not get side-tracked by issues or details that won't assist the main goal of recovery. After all, the disordered eater is barely clinging to life; he/she is unable to process complicated matters, having starved his/her brain beyond recognition. It will require much strength on his/her part to stick to a single goal, like weight gain. Only once weight has been gained, may he/she be equipped to deal with the root of the problem.

"As such," Broughton says, "a detailed treatment plan is important. It is my belief that the treatment plan is the guiding document to keep everyone on the same page—a very important factor in working with someone who suffers from an eating disorder."

Role of Family

It's important for family members to be supportive without enabling. "A very difficult task," says Broughton, "as the loved one is usually an expert at manipulating those who care for them most."

Support can be exhibited by trusting the treatment professionals and their regimen. It can also be shown through verbal encouragement and thoughtful gifts, as well as time spent visiting, watching

TV together and simply *being*. One must be careful, however, not to engage in enabling behaviors such as aligning oneself with the patient against the treatment team.

"This disease is very tough, and will do anything to survive," says Broughton. "It is very easy for the family to believe their loved one about how horrible the facility is, or how horrible the doctor is, or how unfairly and badly they are being treated. These are tools of the disease to distract everyone from fighting it."

Eating disorders, Broughton adds, are experts at triangulating family, friends and the treating professionals.

Families should not belittle their loved ones with examples of past behavior, continuing to hold it over their heads. "Keeping a positive, future focus is important," stresses Broughton.

Treat the person as normal, and don't fixate on food issues. Focus, instead, on recovery, the person's assets, potential, and behaviors that continue the journey. "Like the old adage, 'Catch 'em being good,' and emphasize that."

In the Long Run

Long-term healing takes place one day at a time, and is hastened by avoiding people, places, things and behaviors that act as triggers.-

"Realistically, no one can avoid all the things in the past that initiated and perpetuated the disease," says Broughton. As a result, support systems are extremely important. These may consist of family, friends, treatment professionals and groups specific to the individual's needs.

Yet support groups pose a danger, as well. "I once worked with a lady who went to a support group for people whose loved ones had committed suicide," Broughton recalls. "She would tell me about the meetings, and I soon discovered it was merely a place where the individuals wallowed in self-pity rather than recovery."

Broughton urges individuals desiring healing to find groups that focus on the future instead of the past, dwelling on positive thoughts and moving forward in continued recovery.

The Counselor's Case

Letting Go

Waiting for a disordered eater to choose recovery is excruciatingly hard, Thompson says, for it requires letting go and trusting God, even as your child seems to be deciding to die.

"We must respect each other's choices even when those choices break our hearts. We are never in control of others' choices anyway. We can only control what goes on within our own skin—almost everything else that happens is beyond our control."

We need to accept this, he says, hard as it may be. "If we can't, then maybe we are attached to the relationship in a way that needs detaching."

One must also learn to resist the actual power struggle, urges Thompson, who trains pastors caring for eating-disordered parishioners. "We can feel sad about what is happening, but still be active in bringing redemption to the situation. Passivity is never helpful. We can always be meaningfully and actively involved, and then the feelings of helplessness are usually tolerable."

Learning How to Help

When your loved one finally chooses to recover, it is imperative *not* to focus on food, exercise or body image, Thompson says. By addressing these topics, you will only increase the power struggle.

Instead, "focus on validating the God-given image and identity of the child. Work at repairing and developing the relationship. Listen to the child's heart, even if it expresses rage and frustration. Honor that expression as God would, and listen."

He also agrees with Broughton's suggestion to surround recovering eaters with community, so they feel loved and valued.

"You can encourage [your loved one] by being engaged in relationship. Whatever you can give is important—presence, tears, tangible support, and even at times, a word from God."

Keep looking through a 30-year window, he adds, versus a 30-day one. "Pray to see things through God's eyes."

No matter if the individual relapses, there is always the hope that God never stops working to bring a Christian to maturity, "and that includes eating disordered children."

However, the child must receive what God has to give. "Some *do* die of the disease—we can't hide from that fact. However, we *can* have faith that God will see all of the complexities and never stop doing what can be done."

God loves the disordered eater even more than we do, Thompson insists, "and we can fellowship with Him in His suffering."

Seeing Through Eyes of Faith

Even when it seems your child is choosing death; even when the road to recovery is full of potholes, "We don't see all that God is doing," says Thompson, "so we need to look through eyes of faith."

No matter how dire our situation, God is good. And there is nothing that can change that. "The story is not finished. The story line may change tomorrow, next year, or even 20 years from now."

While outer healing may seem to be occurring slowly, God is healing on the inside. "We never really know what is going on inside another; there can be many things being done to heal the internal pain in the heart of the anorexic."

It often takes a long time for the story to unfold. Yet, there *is* hope, Thompson insists. Over the years, he's not only observed Emily's recovery; he's also witnessed God appearing at a critical moment in other disordered eaters' lives, changing their sense of identity and inspiring a journey to healing.

Additionally, "I've seen a death in the family break the hardness of heart that was keeping a [disordered eater] bound," he continues. "I've seen concerted prayer break Satan's lies or strongholds. [And] I've seen communities come around a [disordered eater] because of God's leading, and bring miraculous healing."

Switching Identities

When asked whether or not he believes complete healing from an eating disorder is possible, Thompson defers to 1 Corinthians 6:9-11, which says, "Do you not know that the wicked will not inherit the kingdom of God? Do not be deceived: Neither the sexually immoral nor idolaters nor adulterers nor male prostitutes nor homosexual offenders nor thieves nor the greedy nor drunkards nor slanderers nor swindlers will inherit the kingdom of God. *And that is what some of you were.* But you were washed, you were sanctified, you were justified in the name of the Lord Jesus Christ and by the Spirit of our God."

That verse, he says, implies that in Christ, our identity is changed. And as far as God is concerned, one is no longer an anorexic or a bulimic, etcetera, but God's child—washed, sanctified and justified.

"Will a sanctified saint struggle with temptation at times? Probably—but her identity is not that of a disordered eater. She has been changed into the likeness of Christ and reflects His character deep in her soul."

Chapter 16

Prayer

Abba Father,

THANK YOU FOR BEING here with us. We praise Your Name. Thank You for always hearing our prayers, and for so faithfully sustaining us over the past months and years. Thank You for sending Your Son to die for us, for redeeming us daily, even hourly, and for leading us gently into salvation.

LORD, we ask You to forgive our many sins. We ask that You'd meet us where we're at, and show us how we've wronged both You and our loved ones. Forgive us, Father, for harsh words said; for times when we've stepped ahead of Your Holy Spirit, and for moments in which we've held back in fear. Forgive us, LORD, for the moments we've despaired, and for those in which we've assumed to know better than You. Cleanse our hearts so they might be found pleasing in Your sight.

God, we thank You and give You praise for _____ who has decided to walk the path to recovery. We give You the glory for this, LORD. You knew this day would come. We praise You for sustaining _____'s life, and ask that You would continue to minister to him/her.

Now, more than ever, be present as he/she walks this new road. Protect _____ from the evil one. Give _____ discernment to know what choices to make. Sustain and lead _____ over the coming months and years, as he/she chooses to walk in the light. And keep him/her from fear.

Guide us, LORD, as we seek to encourage and uplift _____ on this healing journey. Help us know what to say and do. Give us wisdom, and fill our hearts with patience and love. We realize this will not be an easy process, but we praise You because You are redeeming our loved one from the grips of an eating disorder, and for this, we are thankful. We dedicate his/her life to You. We ask that You would use him/her for Your glory, and for Your Name's sake.

Fill us with your strength. Heal those of us who are hurting, and give us grace to walk now, with our loved one, on the path to victory. Keep the enemy at bay. Protect all of us from his schemes and wishes. Make us Your humble servants, LORD, and keep us ever close to Your side.

Thank You, again, for what You've done in our lives through this process, and for what You're about to do. Be with us now.

In Jesus' Holy Name we pray,

Amen.

Part IV

RENEWAL

*How to help a loved one
walk in healing*

Chapter 17

Grown-Up Child's Perspective

My Story

I WAS CLEANING OUT my refrigerator when I found them: two muffin bottoms. I paused, holding the zip-lock bag in my hand, recalling the two lunches in which I'd allowed myself the top, but not the bottom of a single muffin, with a couple slices of cheese. That was one week ago. *Really?* I thought to myself. *After all this time, am I still a disordered eater?*

It had been four years since my last battle with anorexia. I had a baby now, and had been eager to lose the baby weight—a little bit too eager. It had been all too easy to slide back into regimented eating.

I'd found it easier to justify eating while pregnant. But herein lay the problem. I felt I had to excuse it by having a baby inside of me.

It would have been selfish *not* to eat, I thought, for that would have meant starving my unborn child. But I still had yet to learn, it was selfish to withhold food from my own body, simply for the sake of loving myself.

Compliments abounded while I was pregnant: "You are so beautiful!" and "Wow, you look good," because I had covered up my jagged edges. But even after all this time, I still believed I looked better a certain size—a smaller size—and that it was worth denying my body nourishment in order to achieve it.

Eating wasn't supposed to be this difficult; I knew that. But I also knew, eating (or not eating) wasn't the problem. It was merely a physical means for coping with underlying spiritual issues. Specifically:

Control. In order to walk in renewal, I needed to admit I couldn't control all of life's elements, and that I didn't need to try (through stringent eating), for God knew each of my days before they came to be. And this was more than enough. In addition to admitting this on a daily basis, I needed to relinquish my desire for control, and to risk submitting myself into God's capable hands.

Guilt. Being a people-pleaser, I suffered enormous bouts of guilt over issues long forgiven and forgotten. To combat this guilt, I would punish myself by not eating enough. Yet, a renewed mind feeds off grace, not guilt, and so I needed to forgive myself—again, on a daily basis—before I'd be free to eat.

Anger. With such high expectations of myself, I also suffered from constant disappointment in others; not only was I playing "god" by deeming how they should and shouldn't respond; I was using anorexia as a means of self-protection, so my heart would harden and I wouldn't get hurt.

In order to walk renewed, I needed to forgive those who'd hurt me in the past, to relinquish my desire to play god, and to accept that humanity was imperfect. I had to learn to place my trust in God, not in man, for He would never let me down.

Self-hatred. I had never liked the way I looked. I didn't like the way God had made me. I wished to be small and petite, whereas my body type was tall and curvy. When I was young, I had decided that, instead of being jealous of what others looked like, I would do everything I could to look the way they did, for jealousy was futile. In doing so, I made a kind of covenant to alter the person God had made me.

Instead of trying to change myself, I should have embraced who I was. It's impossible to walk in renewal if you are continually holding on to that other "self," the person you wish you were. I needed to accept who God had made me, big bones and all, and to allow Him, instead of dieting, to shape me.

It would take realizing these issues, and committing them to God each morning, for my mind to be renewed.

"I'm trying so hard," I insisted to a friend one day.

"But I'm afraid that one day you'll get tired of trying," my friend responded, "and then the anorexia will return."

Renewal requires more than physical wellness or personal effort; it begs for divine intervention, in order to deal with the spiritual issues that caused the disease in the first place.

Pregnant Dreams

Every day I am being healed. Every day, I choose to eat three healthy meals. Not only for myself, but for my husband, and, as of November 12, 2009, for our miracle baby—Aiden Grey—a baby who should have never been, according to the doctors, yet somehow, is.

I credit the miracle to a prayer uttered by a pastor. A pastor who'd heard my testimony on *100 Huntley Street*—my story of how God had healed me from anorexia—and the fact that, in spite of my healing, doctors had still said I'd probably never give birth.

Following my live performance on May 12, 2008, this pastor, who had also appeared on the show that day, offered to pray for Trent and me. After we conceded, he and his wife lay hands on us in the back room of the studio, asking God to give us a son within the year.

I wondered at the specificity, but appreciated the effort. Three months later, I conceived. While the line on the pregnancy test stick was faint, our joy was bold. We delighted in a God who does the impossible. We placed hands on my womb at night, dreaming of pudgy feet and loving our little Papoose.

Then, on October 6, the blood—bold as our joy had been. I could do nothing but sit on the couch and cry. And my husband could do nothing but hold me.

Soon after my miscarriage, precancerous cells were discovered in my cervix, and so, a dim light shone. I found solace in saying, "See, God had a reason for this." But God has a reason for everything, even for situations without silver linings.

While I took extra care to eat well, drink right and sleep long; while Trent and I began to again to try to conceive, I secretly gave up hope of having my own children, convinced the doctors had been right. I knew, however, that God wanted me, somehow, to be a mother, for the day the placenta left my body I opened my Bible and found myself staring at this verse: "He settles the barren woman in her home as a happy mother of children." (Psalm 113:9)

And so, we began foster care training. Then, when the opportunity arose to adopt a local baby boy due in May—the same month we'd expected to give birth—we saw it as a sign. But after the papers had been signed and the process was underway, the mother changed her mind. Again, soul-gutting pain. Much like the miscarriage.

In spite of the tears, I heard His voice, saying, "I settle the barren woman..." And in March of 2009, not long after the mother had changed her mind, I discovered I was five weeks pregnant. Not quite one year after the pastor had prayed. This time, the line on the stick was bright pink. While our joy was hesitant, it became bolder as the weeks passed and my womb bulged with new life.

And on November 12, 2009, we gave birth—messy, miraculous birth—to a beautiful, bright-eyed son, Aiden Grey.

God gives, and He takes away, and He gives again. Life holds seasons of despair, and seasons of joy. I didn't know why He chose to honor that pastor's prayer and give me a son. I, of all people, don't deserve the wordless wonder of being a parent. I, who once starved my body and wished only to become skinnier. I, who held no respect for the body's curves and its creative power. Yet our God is a God of grace.

"Every good and perfect gift... comes down from the Father," the book of James tells us. In this, is our hope. In this, is our future.

God, the Father, knows our dreams to conceive. He also knows what it means to lose a child. And when He did, the earth cracked, the temple's curtain tore, and the sky split in a fury of tears. He was angered and saddened and made sore by the unfairness of it all. But three days later, new life arose.

We cannot know the hows, nor the whens nor the whys. But we *can* know a God who is bigger than our problems, a God who delights in giving good gifts to His children. And one day, in *His* sovereign timing, we will give birth to the dreams He's planted within us.

Personally Speaking

I believe in full recovery, but I also believe it is only possible through God's supernatural power, and that it is necessary to choose this healing, every day. Anorexia is a mental illness, so I need to let God renew my mind daily. And in order to do that, I need to walk in holiness and in light, avoiding the shadows where calories and scales and mirrors lurk.

I find it's easiest to choose healing when I think about all of the people who love me. When I consider my husband, my (now two) sons, my parents, my siblings, my in-laws and my friends—what a "great cloud of witnesses," says Hebrews 12:1.

And so, with this in mind, I "throw off everything that hinders and the sin that so easily entangles, and … run with perseverance the race marked out for us." Isn't this what Christianity is about? Living for others?

Yes, we must love ourselves, but only on account of others. It is for others that Christ lay down His life. And, in the same respect, it is for others that I choose life, each day, so God might use me for His glory.

The temptations are still there, and some days are easier than others. Some days it takes all my will to rise from bed and be obedient. And some days, I fail. I stumble into self-pity and forget *Whose* I am.

But then I stare down at the smooth cheeks of my small boy feeding, at the way he swallows life-giving manna-milk flowing white from my chest and I cry. Then I slice homemade bread and slather it with jam and butter and eat because, in eating, I produce life. Not only spiritually or emotionally, but physically. And this is a miracle.

Love on a Platter

I am fortunate to have a husband who says he trusts me, in spite of my relapse. His very trusting makes me want to please him.

Sometimes it's easiest to deceive the ones who love you, because they want most to believe in you. But my husband still believes in me. He asks me what I've eaten some days, yet he never nags; just reminds me that he loves me the way God made me.

As a former anorexic walking in renewal, I would highly recommend eating as though there *were* a child living inside of you, until you're able to love yourself enough to eat for *you*—which is what we should all be striving for. After all, the Bible says the Holy Spirit makes our bodies His temple.

Acknowledging this life within us will keep us in tune with our body's cravings; it will inspire us to study nutrition, to understand what our bodies need in order to thrive, and it will help us to honor and respect the vessel God has given us.

If a menu will keep you on track, and keep you from thinking about food more than necessary, then scrawl down some meal ideas on paper and pin it to your refrigerator.

But don't be stuck to that paper. Free yourself to learn how to eat in a spontaneous way that has nothing to do with measuring cups or weigh scales. Dare to eat a bowl of ice cream once in a while, or something that isn't entirely "healthy," as an act of sacrifice to God. As you eat it, say, "See Lord, I trust you."

Become re-acquainted with your body, and fall in love with the person God made you to be. Then, food will be put back in its rightful place: instead of being an obsession, it will become a means of worshiping the creator, by honoring his creation (you!). Nothing more; nothing less.

Accountability

Trent and I enjoy the sitcom, *Seinfeld*. There's one episode in which George decides to start doing the opposite of what he'd normally do each day, because his "normal" self cannot be trusted to make the right choices.

In the same way, I've learned I cannot rely upon myself. My first instinct, still, is to schedule out my meals, divide up portions, and count calories. So, three times a day, I do the opposite of what I would normally do, and force myself past that first instinct so that I'm able to enjoy a meal.

While I cannot always be trusted, I want to become trustworthy. I want for Opposite Emily to become Every-Day Emily. With this in mind, having an accountability partner outside of home will keep you true to yourself and to your partner.

I chose a woman from church who, prior to having kids, also battled anorexia.

Being retired, she had the time to devote to me, and having struggled with eating, she was sympathetic. But not only that; she was a believer, whose relationship with her husband I deeply respected. As a result, I wanted to learn from her. We were able to pray together, and she, to teach me how to be a better wife and mother.

Art Therapy

I am an artist. I always have been—sketching, playing with pastels and charcoals and other mediums—but now, I paint. Oils, acrylics—it doesn't matter. I slather them on thick, and create beauty on canvas. I use bright colors, for in them, I find simplicity and hope. The same kind of childlike wonder that manifests itself each spring in the light green of tree, the dark fringe of moss on creek bed; the blood red of tulip, the singing yellow of daffodils and daisies; and sky splashing blue across the heavens.

I make art because, in it, I find meaning. There's peace in knowing I am more than this mortal skin. More than this body, which so often causes me heartache. As I make art, I transcend weight and scales and calories, and I rest. In knowing I was made for a reason—to create—even as much as I've been created. These fingers, these eyes, which let me do art, were formed by my God. And I am unique, even as my painting is one-of-a-kind.

Maybe you don't paint. But I encourage you to find some way of creating. Some form of molding, making, or being, which forces you beyond the superficial. Which allows you to be "free," even for a moment. Through song, guitar, chalk on sidewalk, knitting, tie-dying silks or sewing dresses, transcend yourself; escape your thoughts, and get involved with something greater.

Art forces us to go beyond ourselves, to commune with the other. To act selflessly, through creation, abandoning negativity and choosing to believe in something positive.

In this is the secret to healing. In escaping ourselves, and choosing to live for Someone Else. In believing we were made for more than a disease. In believing our identity is entwined with the Creator's.

We have a divine purpose. We are framed masterpieces, on display for the world to see, and through our pictures—which are perfect, in spite of their flaws—people see the Heavenly Artist. And they weep for His beauty.

Learn to Love Me

Every day I seek the Word for my worth. I do this to under-stand—to truly "get"—how valuable I am. It's as though I'm learn-ing a new language, a holy way of speaking, and as with any schooling, it takes practice to make perfect.

Slowly, I am becoming fluent in verses like, "I am fearfully and wonderfully made; your works are wonderful, I know that full well." (Psalm 139:14) Slowly, my insides are beginning to reverberate with these truths. But the voice of the enemy is ever-present and so, I need to stay familiar with the whisper of scripture's translucent pages.

As well, I pray, for in prayer I find God speaking to me, telling me His heart, things spoken in simple glory, and I find meaning in this relationship we share.

Not My Own

My body is not my own. It was bought at a price. I've been told this since I was a little girl, but only recently understood. Having given birth, I can now see the dichotomy of purity emerging from red slimy innards of human flesh, the perfection of a baby's toes, the heaven-splitting smile which widens child's lips from within my womb, and I know the cost, for it made me scream and bleed and want to die, but I've forgotten this in the joy of being a mother.

And so, I live in renewed awe of my body. I feed it, because it deserves to be fed. I feed it, because God makes temple-presence in-side of me, beating heart in time with heaven-drums that pummel praise to His eternity. I feed it, because I love Him who died for me.

(And what if my child were to choose to starve him/herself, after the price I'd paid to bring him/her to life? It would rip my heart in two. I bleed for you mothers who've had to watch your little one reject the gift you gave. And I pray, alongside you, spirit wobbly and knees aching but praying, for healing and for answers.)

Healing Steps

The Bible says that if we resist the devil, he will flee. Every morning, it's a matter of waking up in my Christ-identity; of silencing the negative whisper that sounds through television ads, magazines and song lyrics; of tuning in to the affirming words of Scripture.

While God assures us that we *are* beautifully and wonderfully made (Psalm 139), He is also quick to remind us that true beauty comes from within: the beauty of a gentle and quiet spirit. (1 Peter 3:4)

Now, I seek to bring confidence and beauty into my home as wife, mother, daughter, sister, artist and writer. I beg God daily to give me wisdom within each of these roles, not wanting to drag down my sons or husband with deflated ego, not wanting to pity myself, not wanting to believe anything save the truth.

Some days are easier than others. Some days I catch the enemy speaking lies into my ear, lies about self-worth and body image, but I refuse to believe them. Having learned what his voice sounds like— the slithering, deceptive hiss of a snake—I drown it out with Scripture, letting God's holy, healing word mend the parts of me still broken, asking Him to give me the strength to focus on others, not myself.

For it is in this brokenness, this imperfection, that I find grace, and it is by grace that we are saved.

In Short

Instead of trying so hard to be in control, shouldn't we be more afraid of missing out on life as God intended it to be? As often as we mess up, He forgives, but "Don't use this freedom as an excuse to do whatever you want to do and destroy your freedom" (Galatians 5:14). No one knows the hour in which God will call us home.

Chapter 18

Spouse's Perspective

Trent's Story

IT WAS THE THIRD night Emily hadn't slept. Tossing, turning, she finally resorted to the couch, reminding Trent of days long past; days he'd thought his wife had recovered from.

Is she eating well? Trent wondered. And he prayed about how to broach the subject.

The next morning, he found Emily contrite at the breakfast table, eyes red. Head bent. "I don't think I've been eating enough," she confessed. "I'm sorry, Trent. I need to have more protein during the day so I sleep better at night. Please forgive me."

And as she bit down into a piece of toast and peanut butter, Trent breathed deep. Even though she still struggled, Emily was now open, honestly admitting blunders, wanting to walk in healing. And this, he respected.

"I have to trust her, because I can't eat for her," Trent says. "Even when she was in the throes of anorexia, I had to trust that God was going to get her through it. Anything is possible with God, including full recovery."

Trent's Story

Learn to Listen

Not only is it important for a husband to listen to his wife; he needs to encourage her to listen to herself.

When Emily became pregnant in March of 2009, she let down all guards and began trusting her body completely. "She made a very conscious effort to listen to her body, and to give it what it needed," Trent says. "She really wanted to be healthy for her baby, so that was very encouraging."

Emily became re-acquainted with her physical being, learning what it craved, whether it was protein, calcium or fruit, and she obeyed, giving in, respecting her physical instincts.

And this, Trent believes, is one of the keys to renewal. This learning to listen to the body's voice.

Make Food Fun

Having grown up on a farm, Trent holds a very pragmatic view of food. "We were at the production stage of it," he says. "I knew where food came from; we grew it and ate our own produce. Food wasn't just a means to an end; it was a way of life. We were feeding people—grain for bread, cows for beef—so food was our livelihood. And we knew food was good. It was never something to be feared."

This freedom from fear, Trent believes, is essential to living in renewal. One cannot enjoy healing while obsessing about size or quantity or measurement. One can only be healed after embracing food for what it is—a gift to unwrap.

To not enjoy food, Trent says, is a sin. "God gave us food in the beginning. He could have had us not eat, or survive some other way, but He gave us food to enjoy. Jesus was accused of being a glutton and a drunkard, which shows He enjoyed partaking in a meal."

One can still make healthy choices, Trent adds, but it's important to let loose and eat a piece of chocolate cake, or a butter tart, in celebration of God's gift.

Admit Struggles

Renewal requires little steps. And Trent delights in taking those little steps alongside his wife. "I know now, she wants to be well—and that's what matters."

He has learned to be honest about his own struggles; in return, Emily confides in him, knowing he won't judge her or command her to change.

Even though Emily still has bad days, "She realizes when she's messing up now, and she talks openly about it with me," says Trent. "She admits when she hasn't eaten enough, so I can trust she's looking after herself."

A SPOUSE'S ROLE
Feed the Family

Trent desires wholeness, not only for his wife, but for his family.

Together, he and Emily talk about ways to inspire health and confidence within their boys. "I think we should build up self-esteem in our children—compliment them, and make them feel loved and accepted," says Trent. "I don't want to count calories or be worried about food. Rather, I think we should just serve healthy meals—with our children dishing up their own plates—and not let them eat a bunch of junk food."

They've both committed to eating every meal, and to celebrating food as a family. "I want food to bring us together, not drive us apart," Trent says.

They also hope to demonstrate freedom when it comes to eating. "We'll make smart choices, but we won't be afraid to have bacon or ice cream once in a while."

Love Her

When helping one's wife to walk in renewal, Trent urges husbands to be gentle in their approach.

"Be very loving when you talk about food, because it's a sensitive subject," he says. "It's important to let them know that you're there to support them, not control them, and to let them know you trust them. You can't be watching them all the time, so you have to trust."

Keep a closed mouth, he says, and an open door. "Let your wife know if she is struggling, she can talk about it with you anytime, and you won't judge her."

But urge her to walk in healing. "Encourage your wife to make the right decisions," Trent says, "and expect that she will."

Chapter 19

Professional Perspective

AS A DISORDERED EATER learns to walk in renewal, careful steps are required.

While it's possible to fully recover, and to obtain a new identity in Christ, it's also possible to relapse. In order to keep from raising one's family or loved ones in fear of food, and in order to walk in true healing and wholeness, please prayerfully heed the professional advice below.

The Doctor's Diagnosis

Disordered Parenting

When it comes to advising former disordered eaters in the renewing of the mind, Broughton draws on research done by Dr. Judy Scheel, Founder and Executive Director of Cedar Associates—a private outpatient program for eating disordered patients.

Disordered eating will lead to disordered parenting, says Scheel. "Eating-disordered mothers will often have issues around their children's food," she writes in her pamphlet, *Early Intervention is Key*. Severe cases, she continues, tell of children failing to thrive because of anorexic mothers restricting their food intake.

"Less severely, mothers report an array of feeding behaviors with their children, including rigidity about meals and treats, and no structure—permitting children to have whatever, whenever."

Maternal anxiety around feeding may interfere with the mother's sense of competence in caring for her child, Scheel continues. This sense of ability is essential in maternal-child bonding. "Mothers who feel incompetent are subject to daily assaults to their self-esteem, and are deprived of the joy and fun of raising a child."

Incompetent, fearful eaters risk damaging their children in a number of ways, including:

A child's sense of autonomy. It is cyclical. A mother's perception of food affects her child's, even if it is subconscious.

"We have seen teenagers and adults who have difficulty accepting that they have an eating disorder because the behavior is one they grew up witnessing," writes Scheel. "It seems 'normal' to them. Even if the child does not develop an eating disorder, the child of an eating-disordered parent may be more likely to use food to cope with uncomfortable feelings as they grow up."

A mother's abnormal need to control food—by restricting her child's portions even when he/she is still hungry, or being rigid about eating meals at certain times—may hinder or suppress a child's ability to self-feed, affecting his/her sense of mastery, self-esteem and autonomy.

"The inability to be in tune with the child's needs because of [a mother's] own issues around food [will] create confusion for the child," says Scheel. Feeling confused about one's own needs can form the bedrock for a variety of other difficulties in one's child.

Imbalance. A mother who soothes herself by binging on sweets will teach a child that he/she can turn to food to resolve one's problems.

In the same way, withholding treats because a child is "bad," or starving oneself to numb the pain will foster feelings of deprivation and sadness within the child. "The importance of helping the mother to have balance and comfort in her relationship to food becomes clear," writes Scheel.

The Attachment Theory

The Attachment Theory, formed by John Bowlby (1907-1990), states that a child's attachment to caregivers is a fundamental determinant of the strength of the child's later relationships.

"Where there is a secure core state, a person feels good about themselves and their capacity to be effective and pursue their projects," says Bowlby. "Where the core state is insecure, defensive strategies come into play."

Loss of Attachment

According to Scheel, loss of attachment can manifest itself in a number of ways:

- Living in a household where the child is frequently criticized.
- Not valuing a child for who he/she is and expecting him/her to live up to the parental/familial ideal.
- Parent's untreated depression, substance abuse, or eating disorder (which consumes the parent, leaving little availability to the child).
- Envy by the parent toward the child, which often leaves the child feeling guilty and ashamed of their needs and anything good that comes their way, or which they create or manifest in life.
- Unresolved conflicts from a parent's own childhood, which cause and perpetuate problems in their relationship with their own children.
- Absence of an emotional language in the family, which leaves a child feeling unable to connect with their emotions and internal states and creates a chasm (detachment) between parent and child. (i.e., The family that utilizes the "pull yourself up by the bootstrap" approach or the "fix it" approach rather than identifying, feeling and expressing emotions as the means to feel better and maintain safety with and connection to family members.)

In each scenario, the loss of emotional connection results in a lessening of the ability for a child to form a connection and experience of a stable core self.

This lack of identity can therefore propel itself into an eating disorder, which provides a strong sense of self, an attachment to some "thing," as well as "a symbolic container" for everything the sufferer has grown to detest about him/herself (i.e., needs and wants, hunger for love and understanding, comfort and closeness).

Coping Mechanisms
Vertical Connections

Dr. Amy Wasserbauer, the former Assistant Clinical Director at Remuda Ranch's adult center who is currently working in higher education as a psychologist as well as in a private practice, has helped numerous disordered eaters on the path to recovery. The most important step one can take towards healing, she believes, is establishing a vertical connection, or quiet time, with God.

"The anorexic person [especially] tends to be more driven, more performance-perfection focused, so allowing it to be a contemplative time, a time that's foundational to setting the focus of the day—also, a time of honest confession of struggles and urges—keeps them grounded."

Accountability

Secondly, she says, there's the need for accountability. She and her friend, who is in recovery from anorexia, have spoken together once a week for the past 10 years. Being a mother of small children, "Her prayer request is for time, space with God to settle her spirit, to not get anxious." And Wasserbauer is able to lift her friend up in prayer, each week, knowing these specifics.

Part of this accountability means keeping a diary card. Each week, patients are to record their thoughts in the diary, then allow a dietitian and therapist to read it.

"It's a daily check-in for emotions, urges, and skill usage," says Wasserbauer.

And it's skill usage that unlocks the door for renewal.

Saving Skills

"Skill usage is the train track to treatment and recovery," says Wasserbauer. "You have to have a way to replace the behavior, so our goal is to treat the person by replacing how they coped before—giving them a new way to deal with life."

Whether they're interpersonal effectiveness skills, emotional regulation skills, or practicing presence skills, it's important to exercise them daily. Yet, they will not give the same endorphins as an eating disorder; one will not receive a "high" by applying skills to their life. Rather, these skills renew one's mind, therefore offering hope, healing and help on days when life seems out of control.

"You may have bad body image days," says Wasserbauer; "days when you feel like you've gained hundreds, but that's not a reality. So how do you allow that to become an alarm clock? Emotional regulation skills allow eating disorder urges to serve as an alarm clock; you then do a feelings check, and look into your heart and ask, 'What's really going on?'"

Behavior Chain Analysis

In addition to applying these skills, one needs to do a Behavior Chain Analysis. "If it's a hard morning, and a former anorexic person has the urge to restrict because maybe they overslept or got in a traffic jam or got chewed out, and suddenly it's noon and they don't want to eat, they can analyze their behavior," explains Wasserbauer.

1. What made me vulnerable to the eating disorder? (i.e., had a bad dream; woke up late; is having a 'bad image day')
2. What were my triggers today? (i.e., traffic jam; got chewed out)
3. What were my thoughts, feelings, and behaviors? (i.e., feeling depressed, so I'm not going to eat today)

"Our goal is to teach them how to build skills so they don't follow through with the behavior—to learn at any point they have the capability to break the chain with God's help," explains Wasserbauer.

One skill application would be to call a friend and confess, then choose to eat, thereby breaking the chain.

Another option would be to work on becoming present in the moment, versus anxious about the future, by focusing on the five senses.

"Behavior chains and skill integration may be necessary every day," Wasserbauer says. "Renewal may take a long time, but nevertheless, just ask, "For this day, how do I practice staying in the moment?'"

Balanced Home

When it comes to raising children in health and wholeness, Wasserbauer says it's crucial for parents to be a team. "Both parents have accountability—not just Mom, who's had the eating disorder," she says.

Mom needs to work at loving herself on a daily basis, Wasserbauer continues. "Self-love as a whole is top priority. That is the greatest commandment—to love your neighbor as yourself. The call to love our children comes out of our ability to accept ourselves, and to accept God's love."

Fathers need to support their wives in this initiative, and to stop critiquing people, both in and out of the family, in regards to their size. "So many of our patients have been affected by their father's and grandfather's perceptions of food," says Wasserbauer. "They're so food focused."

Do not discuss body image issues with your children. Also, "get rid of the word 'healthy.'" And do not use food as a means of controlling your children, or appeasing your own guilt.

Guide your little ones in their portions, and teach them what it means to feel "satisfied," but don't create harsh restrictions (such as one cookie a day) or allow them to eat anything they want; instead, encourage them to know their bodies, and to know when they've had enough. In other words, teach them intuitive eating.

Intuitive Eating

Remuda Ranch bases its nutritional philosophy on the book, *Intuitive Eating*, by Evelyn Tribole, M.S., R.D., and Elyse Resch, M.S., R.D., F.A.D.A.

"There is no good food or bad food," summarizes Wasserbauer, who worked closely with the nutrition staff during her period as team leader at Remuda. "We don't rank food. We enjoy it. The goal is to not be afraid of food—we have control over it."

It's okay to let your children not finish their plates, she says. Just teach them to know when they're full.

Don't go to extremes, and don't label food. Just enjoy your cookie, and your apple. "It's about moderation," says Wasserbauer. "It's about not being afraid that, if I have fries, they're going to kill me."

Following are the 10 Principles of Intuitive Eating:

1. Reject the Diet Mentality

Throw out the diet books and magazine articles that offer you false hope of losing weight quickly, easily, and permanently. Get angry at the lies that have led you to feel as if you were a failure every time a new diet stopped working and you gained back all of the weight.

If you allow even one small hope to linger that a new and better diet might be lurking around the corner, it will prevent you from being free to rediscover intuitive eating.

2. Honor Your Hunger

Keep your body biologically fed with adequate energy and carbohydrates. Otherwise you can trigger a primal drive to overeat. Once you reach the moment of excessive hunger, all intentions of moderate, conscious eating are fleeting and irrelevant. Learning to honor this first biological signal sets the stage for rebuilding trust with yourself and food.

3. Make Peace with Food

Call a truce; stop the food fight! Give yourself unconditional permission to eat. If you tell yourself that you can't or shouldn't have a particular food, it can lead to intense feelings of deprivation that develop into uncontrollable cravings and, often, binging.

When you finally "give-in" to your forbidden food, eating will be experienced with such intensity, it usually results in Last Supper feasting, and overwhelming guilt.

4. Challenge the Food Police

Scream a loud "NO" to thoughts in your head that say you're "good" for eating under 1,000 calories or "bad" because you ate a piece of chocolate cake.

The Food Police monitor the unreasonable rules that dieting has created. The police station is housed deep in your psyche, and its loud speaker shouts negative barbs, hopeless phrases, and guilt-pro-voking indictments. Chasing away the Food Police is a critical step in returning to intuitive eating.

5. Respect Your Fullness

Listen for the body signals that tell you that you are no longer hungry. Observe the signs that show that you're comfortably full. Pause in the middle of a meal and ask yourself how the food tastes, and what is your current fullness level?

6. Discover the Satisfaction Factor

The Japanese have the wisdom to promote pleasure as one of their goals of healthy living. In our fury to be thin and healthy, we often overlook one of the most basic gifts of existence—the pleasure and satisfaction that can be found in the eating experience.

When you eat what you really want, in an environment that is inviting and conducive, the pleasure you derive will be a powerful force in helping you feel satisfied and content. By providing this ex-perience for yourself, you will find that it takes much less food to de-cide you've had "enough."

7. Honor Your Feelings without Using Food

Find ways to comfort, nurture, distract, and resolve your issues without using food. Anxiety, loneliness, boredom, and anger are emo-tions we all experience throughout life. Each has its own trigger, and each has its own appeasement. Food won't fix any of these feelings.

It may comfort for the short term, distract from the pain, or even numb you into a food hangover. But food won't solve the prob-lem. If anything, eating for an emotional hunger will only make you feel worse in the long run. You'll ultimately have to deal with the source of the emotion, as well as with the discomfort of overeating.

8. Respect Your Body

Accept your genetic blueprint. Just as a person with a shoe size of eight would not expect to realistically squeeze into a size six, it is equally as futile (and uncomfortable) to have the same expectation with body size.

But mostly, respect your body, so you can feel better about who you are. It's hard to reject the diet mentality if you are unrealistic and overly critical about your body shape.

9. Exercise—Feel the Difference

Forget militant exercise. Just get active and feel the difference. Shift your focus to how it feels to move your body, rather than the calorie burning effect of exercise.

If you focus on how you feel from working out, such as energized, it can make the difference between rolling out of bed for a brisk morning walk or hitting the snooze alarm. If, when you wake up, your only goal is to lose weight, it's usually not a motivating factor in that moment of time.

10. Honor Your Health

Make food choices that honor your health and taste buds while making you feel well. Remember that you don't have to eat a perfect diet to be healthy. You will not suddenly get a nutrient deficiency or gain weight from one snack, one meal, or one day of eating.

It's what you eat consistently over time that matters. Progress, not perfection, is what counts.

(Excerpt reprinted with permission from www.intuitiveeating.com.)

Healthy Habits

Here are some tips from Wasserbauer on how to raise intuitive eaters:

- Do not label food as good or bad.
- Teach limits.
- Don't foster a dieting mentality.
- Help your children understand "balance."
- Give options—don't force food.
- Learn to let go—find replacements for a particular food if your child doesn't like it.
- Indulge in "unhealthy" foods once in a while.

- Practice moderation.
- Teach freedom in eating—let your children pick recipes or restaurants.
- Always partake in meals with your family.
- Eat together once a day.
- Let your children see you enjoying food.
- Teach your children what it means to wait. "Many of our patients struggle with instant gratification issues," says Wasserbauer. "Children need to learn resilience."
- Help them deal with negative emotions such as frustration or anger. Give your kids permission to feel; teach them how to channel their emotions. "Many (disordered eaters) have turned their anger inward because they didn't know how to cope with it," explains Wasserbauer, "Then, they became depressed and stopped eating because they felt full, emotionally."
- Never obsess over mealtimes.
- Don't be so relaxed that you forget to teach good nutrition.
- Speak positively about your own body, and about others'.

The Nurse's Corner

Rachel Koprowski is a registered nurse who specializes in obesity prevention with the Thames Valley Family Health Team in London, Ontario.

Obesity, she says, is like any eating disorder, in that it's triggered by personality as well as by circumstance.

Koprowski focuses daily on helping families establish balanced, nutritional eating within the home. Following are some observations she's made over the course of her career.

Abusive Scenarios

When it comes to food abuse, "Many times, these types of situations are set against the backdrop of broken families," Koprowski says.

Often, this will lead to attitudes such as, "There isn't enough money for healthy food choices," or "I don't have the time to cook healthy foods—processed or pre-packed is faster," or "I'm too tired to fight with my kids over food; they can have whatever they want." (The parent becomes a short-order cook, often choosing what is fast over a balanced meal.)

While the actual situations are distinctly unique, they can include children who binge on unhealthy foods when their parents are away; children who request fast food on a daily basis, knowing their parents are exhausted and vulnerable; or children who snack on foods high in sugar, salt and unhealthy fats.

"For this reason, establishing a healthy culture within the family at a very early age is essential to circumventing problems later on."

Avoiding Food Abuse

When it comes to preventing eating disorders, Koprowski encourages parents to establish a home life in which positive patterns of eating, activity and communication skills are modeled and imparted to their children.

"The power of the home life cannot be underestimated," she says. "It is here that the frame of reference through which they see the world and themselves is established."

Tips for a healthy home include:

Having family meals together. "Family mealtimes are especially important in cultivating both emotional and physical health within the family," says Koprowski. "During such times, however, parents should not focus their energies on making the children eat as much as they should focus on role-modeling healthy eating and exhibiting healthy forms of communication."

Letting children decide when (outside of established family meals) and how much to eat (children often prefer to graze versus stick to three meals a day). "The idea of 'cleaning your plate' puts children in a difficult position, as they are extremely intuitive about when they are hungry *and* when they are full," says Koprowski. "Asking children to take one or two bites of a new food (usually vegetables) that they're initially hostile toward is vastly different than (a) forcing them to eat the whole serving or (b) not expecting them to try new or less favored foods at all."

Purchasing healthy snacks. "I would recommend that parents avoid making unhealthy choices available within the home," Koprowski says. "Children will often gravitate toward the foods higher in salt, unhealthy fats, and/or sugar if presented with these options. Providing a variety of fresh fruits and vegetables with healthy fats and proteins (humus, cheese) is best."

Getting active. Parents should enjoy the beauty of the outside world, thereby encouraging children to discover and to play.

Limiting screen-time. Curb TV time in order to encourage active use of one's imagination, as well as to avoid inundating children with unhealthy perceptions of body image worth and advertisements for junk food.

Communicating with your child. If children don't receive input from parents about how to live in health and wholeness, it will come from other sources, and not necessarily with loving intent.

Spiritually Speaking

Koprowski believes spirituality plays a central role in eating. After all, she says, many food abuses take place without the pervasive conviction that:

1. **I am absolutely loved, cherished and desired by my Creator.**
2. **God invites me into partnership with Him to bring beauty and healing to the earth.**
3. **His Spirit resides in this temple otherwise known as my physical body.**

"Set against this backdrop, there is a new awareness of one's inherent value and a sense of accountability and responsibility that accompanies all physical acts," she says, "including eating."

God wants us to delight in food, Koprowski continues. "He's designed some amazing items!"

Yet we also need to be aware of the many debilitating options available to us in the North American culture. "As our awareness grows, so too does our responsibility to moderate consumption of items which, when eaten on a regular basis, jeopardize our potential to live as free beings, fully alive and reflecting God in His glory."

The Counselor's Case

Soul Factor

Brookhaven Hospital chaplain Bernard Hubbard believes eating disorders—and their subsequent recovery—stem from the soul.

"The root always produces the fruit," says Hubbard. "The root of the disorder is in the soul (mind, will, emotions), and expresses itself through the body."

Hubbard believes the illness plants itself within the soul through a series of unpleasant words, events or negative thoughts. "Instead of casting the negative thoughts out, many people bury them as a seed in their heart," he says.

"This seed then grows into a false belief system, and becomes the person's reality." As the negativity is allowed to continue, the emotional pain intensifies, and the eating disorder becomes a 'drug of choice' to cope with, control, or divert the pain.

"I have seen how medication and therapy *do* help with the symptoms and working through the facts of their lives," says Hubbard. Yet when it comes to true healing, he adds, "They must deal with the root of the disorder—the negative thoughts that G.R.A.S.P. their soul."

The following chart explains Hubbard's theory.

Facts	Truth	Scripture
Guilt	No guilt	Romans 8
Rejection	Acceptance	Ephesians 1
Abuse	Loved	I John 4
Shame	Righteousness	Romans 5
Pity	Valuable	Psalms 139

In order to walk in renewal, Hubbard believes, one must replace facts with truth: guilt with no guilt; rejection with acceptance;

abuse with the knowledge that they are, in fact, loved; shame with righteousness; and pity with knowing that, in God, they are truly valuable.

Yet the only way to make the truth sink in is through God's Word. "The Scriptures are the only tools I know that can completely change a person's heart," he says. "Meditating on them daily is the best medication for the soul."

For each of the facts and truths listed in his chart, Hubbard has referenced a specific Bible passage. If prayed through daily, these passages have the divine power to alter the human soul, for they contain a heavenly message that is stronger and greater than other people's opinions and unpleasant events.

"The truth changes facts, but facts don't change the truth," says Hubbard.

Thompson's Tactics

When it comes to walking in healing, Thompson urges former disordered eaters to shower their inner selves and their children in love, acceptance and worth.

"Give yourself, and them, healthy choices," he says. "Stay out of power struggles, and concentrate on producing the aroma of Christ in your home."

Producing the fragrance of Christ means more than doing devotions or attending Sunday services. Rather, it requires replacing one's food addiction with an addiction to God.

This will produce a spiritual high, as well as motivation to "focus on being like Christ and encouraging your children to be like Christ—full of love and acceptance."

Remain in a deep love-relationship with God and with others, and concentrate on creating opportunities to live out your calling, "rather than beating a disease."

When it comes to being aware of spiritual and physical pitfalls, each person is unique. "We need to know ourselves in order to know what to guard against," says Thompson.

In short, he adds, live out your new story, your new identity, and your new sense of worth to the Father. Stay in deep relationships with the people God has put in your life, and love well.

Make use of your talents, and pour yourself into creative projects instead of obsessing over recovery.

And lastly, enjoy who you are—because God made you to reflect His power.

Chapter 20

<u>Prayer</u>

DEAR LORD,

WE PRAISE YOU FOR our bodies. For the way You have brought us through the valley, and are daily giving us strength to climb this mountain of renewal. You are the One who's breathed life into our souls. You are the Creator, Re-creator and Mender. Thank You. We cannot say this enough. You've saved us, not only spiritually, but physically. We owe our lives to You.

We beg forgiveness, LORD, for years spent hurting the ones we love. We repent of pride, of not wanting to receive help; of vanity, and idolatry—of worshiping our own image instead of Yours. We're sorry, LORD. So very sorry.

Continue to make us new creations, we pray. Make us new-minded. Sew up our tattered spirits, and stitch together our broken souls, so we might live in wholeness.

Give us strength to fight temptation, each day, LORD. A divine kind of strength that can only come from You. Give us wisdom, to know how to combat Satan's wiles, and to guide our little ones into health and wellness. Give us boldness to walk daily in this new life, and grace, as we seek how to eat, every day.

Make us only aware of others. Give us tender, growing hearts that expand daily for the needs of the world. Make us mindful of how blessed we are, with this over-abundance of food, and make us generous, knowing how to share while keeping our families fed.

We ask that You use these redeemed bodies for Your glory and for Your name's sake. May our healing not be in vain. Use us to bring life wherever we go. To speak uplifting words into the hearts of our children and grandchildren. To release a beautiful fragrance—one that smells of hope and ministers to those who are hurting.

Protect us now, LORD, and keep our children from the presence of the evil one. Protect them from the temptations of a superficial culture. May our homes nurture depth of character, compassion for others, selflessness, and joy. May we be soul-diggers, reaching ever further into Your Word, seeking how to bring Your Kingdom to pass.

You are the Alpha and the Omega, the Beginning and the End. You are the Divine Artist, the Cosmic Parent. And You have made us beautifully, wonderfully. We declare that now, and we choose to believe this, knowing Your presence lives inside us, and that You are greater. Ever greater.

Amen.

Part V

RELATED ACCOUNTS

Stories of healing

Chapter 21

Karen & Constance

Karen's Story

Recognizing

AS A CHILD, KAREN struggled with a low sense of self-worth. "Her dad would not praise her, and her mom would constantly harp on her about her weight, her clothes, etcetera," says Dan of his late wife. "She never felt like she was good enough."

Karen and Dan married young—at 15 and 17 respectively. At the age of 18, following the birth of their second daughter, Constance, Karen began binging and purging. During this time, she and Dan were in counseling with their pastor for other matters. When Karen admitted to being bulimic, the pastor told her she should stop, because bulimia nervosa was not part of God's will. "She respected him enough to stop," Dan recalls.

Still struggling with her weight, Karen continued to diet, but the bulimia itself didn't re-emerge until seven years later, when she had an ovarian cyst that burst. She could no longer hold down food, and had to be rushed to the hospital. For three weeks, Karen wasn't able to eat; every time she tried, she would vomit. Eventually she recovered, but the vomiting continued in secret.

"This event resurrected the whole bulimic cycle," Dan recalls. "She was watching the scale plummet after years of dieting, and the enemy sowed a lie in her mind that she could have the best of both worlds—eating whatever she wanted and still losing weight."

By this time, they had added a son to their family. Despite engaging in bulimic behaviors, Karen looked healthy, and everyone was complimenting her. "My feelings were twofold," says Dan, about her transformation. "Part of me was thinking, *This behavior is wrong*, but my fleshly side was saying, *She's really thinned down and looks good*. But the end didn't justify the means."

It wasn't long until Karen's habit became an obsession that tore their family apart, spiritually, physically, and financially.

"I noticed around nine or 10 years old that there were issues with food," says Grace, the eldest of the two sisters. "I knew that Dad would send Mom to the store with money to buy food, which she did, but by the time she came home she had eaten it. She would hide huge bags of chocolate and other sweets in her purse in the bottom of the hall closet. She would also eat weird things. I remember her making us pancakes for breakfast. She would give us each three, but then she would make a huge stack—probably 15 or so—for herself and put horseradish all over it before she ate it."

Not only did their mother hoard food, Grace recalls, but she also assigned severe rules to the kids' eating habits. "I was angry because she would eat so much and let us have so little," says Grace. "She was crazy about food—about how we would eat it (mouth closed, chewing silently), how quickly we would eat it, not being allowed to drink anything until our food was gone, not being allowed to get up from the table. Dinner was always a chore."

Karen would get angry at Dan when he brought ice cream home for the children, and was constantly warning her kids against overeating.

Meanwhile, she stayed up late at night so that she could raid the kitchen. Eventually, after admitting she had a problem, she agreed to go to Teen Challenge, a Christian recovery program primarily designed for those struggling with substance abuse, illicit sexual activity and other unhealthy behaviors. At the time, with few programs designed for eating disorders, and none that were Christian, Teen Challenge seemed the best option. Karen remained in the program just three weeks, then ran away.

When she returned home, normal family mealtimes continued, with a slight change; Karen started serving dinner buffet-style, the way it had been served at Teen Challenge. After the meal was over, Karen would eat whatever was left. After everyone went to bed, she would stay up and continue eating whatever she could find.

Reacting

"It was not long before I had to start locking cupboards," says Dan.

Grace remembers feeling very confused. "We had locks on the cupboards and the refrigerator, and Mom told us it was because we were eating too much," she says.

The kids were receiving mixed messages. Sweets were not allowed, but their mother would gorge on gallons of ice cream and bags of chocolate all night, and expect her children to clean up the mess in the morning.

"Mom's eating disorder was more important than anything in her life, including us," says Constance.

Karen's destructive behavior was also starting to severely affect their finances. "She was working a good job, but we were not seeing it come home," recalls Grace. "Dad had to go out at nights to find her at salad bars. She was changing price tags on food at the store. She got in trouble with the law, and had a probation officer. We had bought a house, but could no longer afford the mortgage and Dad lost the house. Bill collectors were calling all the time. Dad had to borrow money from his dad, her dad, her mom, and a man from the church. We were very broke."

After three years of this, "I felt very helpless and discouraged," says Dan. While Karen was going for counseling Saturday mornings, she was lying to her husband, telling him the counseling session lasted all day, when instead, she was dating a neighbor in the afternoons.

By this point she was binging and purging 15-20 times a day. She would eat until her leg went numb from pressing against a nerve.

"I would vacillate between feeling sorry for her, being frustrated with her, and being angry," says Dan. The dishonesty and manipulation was particularly difficult. "She would ask me to write checks for her lunch for $3.50, and then alter them, one time for $63.50."

In spite of the devastating impact of Karen's struggle on Dan and his family, however, Dan says he only felt angry at God once. "There was one time after Karen was gone; I was managing the kids by myself, and everything was collectively falling apart. I was beyond my limits, and I became angry at God for one night," Dan says. Nevertheless, his strong faith in God carried him through the toughest years.

Recovery

In August of 1982, Karen decided she would rather leave the family permanently than get help for her disorder. By this point, it was clear she suffered from more than bulimia. While never evaluated by a psychiatrist during this time, the characteristics of her behavior were consistent with Narcissistic Personality Disorder. She seemed wired to put herself first, with little to no concern for how it might hurt those around her. And when it became apparent that she not only wasn't receiving treatment for her illness, but was continuing to have affairs with multiple men, Dan filed for divorce.

"After four years of hell with her, I had checked out," he says. "I did not want to continue, and I felt God was giving me permission to divorce, based on the affairs."

The kids, meanwhile, were relieved their parents had finally separated. "I didn't have to live with her anymore," admits Grace, who was 12 years old at the time, and suffered from poor body image and suicidal tendencies. "I had secretly prayed for them to divorce."

The house quieted down immediately after their mother left, but it would be years before the emotional scars Karen had caused began to heal.

"My forgiveness process was long," says Grace. "The first time I forgave Mom was when I was 14, after I went into counseling. When I was 19, I was going through some more counseling and remembered more things about her, so I had to forgive her again. The next time was when I was 25 or so; I again remembered new things from the past I had to forgive her for. I talked with her, and was truly honest, and that was when we were able to form a deeper relationship."

However, when Grace became a mother for the first time, she says she had to work through even more issues of anger and resentment. "I couldn't understand how my mother could do some of the things she did to us as children," she says. "So [forgiveness] was an ongoing process."

For the most part, Grace did not struggle from any disordered eating while growing up and into early adulthood. However, she admits to going through periods of overeating after having kids, mostly due to stress. Overall, though, she didn't suffer from the unhealthy habits her mother had engaged in—not in the same way her younger sister did, anyway.

Constance's Story

Recognizing

CONSTANCE WAS A CHUBBY BABY, but as she entered her preteen and teen years she thinned out. For the most part, she liked her figure and had a healthy relationship with food. She would occasionally try a diet for a few days, just because others were doing it, but was generally happy with her size and didn't have food issues. When she went to Bible school at the young age of 16, however, all of that changed.

Within the first two months of her first semester at college, Constance packed on 15 pounds. "The weight gain was caused by unusual binging on my part," she recalls, "triggered primarily by my loneliness and insecurity in a new environment."

It was also the first time that she'd had the opportunity to prepare her own meals, and naturally, was drawn to everything she hadn't been allowed to eat at home, such as sugary cereals, cakes, pies and other treats. "I remember how amazing it felt to just pig out on foods I'd always wished I could have," says Constance. "I knew I was a little out of control with food but I was used to eating whatever I wanted without worrying about weight gain. I just hadn't taken into consideration that I was now eating drastically more than I had at home."

In spite of being turned off to disordered eating due to her mother's extreme battle with bulimia, Constance also felt drawn to the behavior when she felt isolated or sad. "In retrospect, probably the biggest impact of my mother's disorder was the lack of time, attention and love she invested in me and my siblings," Constance recalls. "After the breakup of my parents' marriage when I was around 10, she lived her own life in another city, and I was left without a mother for all intents and purposes. I didn't realize this loss was hurting me until many years later. I am quite sure it contributed in an important way to the devastating loneliness I felt at the beginning of my eating disorder."

Following the 15-pound weight gain, Constance threw herself into some pretty restrictive diets, such as the grapefruit diet, and other popular programs. "On one level, I knew these were not good for me," she admits. "I physically hurt after eating nothing but citrus for a few days. But on the other hand, I was only 16, and I lacked wisdom about how to make healthy choices." When the diets didn't work quickly enough, Constance turned to more extreme measures, including laxatives, restricting followed by binge-starve cycles, and more volatile behaviors. Her life—and weight—spiraled out of control.

Reacting

Things got progressively worse, but because Constance was living out-of-state, her family wasn't around to keep her accountable. "There was a semester during which I would have qualified for anorexia," says Constance, "followed by many semesters which involved more binging, occasional purging, and laxatives."

She was aware that she was in trouble, but upon reaching out, found a campus full of Christians who suggested she needed to pray more. "They were missing the other aspects of my struggle," says Constance. "What I really needed most was to believe that I mattered to someone; that they were interested in me and in walking with me through the chaos of my life." Yet no one seemed to want to dig deeper than the surface, and Constance felt completely alone.

After three and a half years of extreme disordered eating, Constance slipped into seven years of controlled chronic dieting, or EDNOS—Eating Disorders Not Otherwise Specified. "I lost weight down to a size I liked; I felt proud of my body, and of my control over binging," she says. "But even with the physical body looking more like I wanted to, I was still a prisoner living in a shame-based 'cage' of an obsession to be thin."

Prior to getting married at the age of 23, she became very promiscuous with a number of different men, due to an intense desire to be noticed; to be connected to someone, however briefly.

At one point during this time Dan came to visit, and she remembers feeling "devoid of life, desperate for things to be different." Constance tried to convey to her father that things weren't going well, but he didn't pick up on the signals.

"I was never alarmed about her weight," Dan admits. "I was actually shocked when she told me that she was dealing with an eating disorder. But then there were times when I would see her, and I would notice that she was really looking thin. Her arms were really skinny, her neck and face. I thought, 'She's battling.' "

Recovery

As the EDNOS continued, Dan began to express concern over Constance's thinness. "I remember talking to her, reminding her of the situation with her mother, telling her more of the story which she was not aware of at the time," he says.

And it was Dan's comments, in addition to those of others, which finally convinced Constance she needed help. "As I began to open my mind to God's truth, I realized that so much of my life was trapped by my fear of gaining a pound. And I realized I wanted more out of life than the hell I was living in—most of which was the negative self-talk inside my head."

After a decade of disordered eating, at the age of 27, Constance prayed what she calls a wimpy but important prayer: "Lord, help me to be willing to be willing to consider thinking about giving this up."

It was small, she says, but it was more than she had uttered up until that point. And it was enough.

Renewal

Today Constance is the founder and CEO of FINDINGbalance, Inc., a Christian non-profit organization aimed at helping people "eat well and live free." She is also the author of *Life Inside the Thin Cage* and *The Art of Being*.

When asked what she wants parents to know about their children who have disordered eating, she says, "One of the most critical things which could have changed my life would have been to have parents who were intentional about engaging with me on an ongoing basis, even after I left home. Our need for parental approval and connection is something we don't grow out of, and it can make an incredible difference in difficult times."

She also encourages parents to get healthy, so they can be there for their kids. "No one is perfect," she says. "We all make mistakes. But if we can be healthy enough to at least talk about what's going on inside of us, and to forgive and encourage and support each other, we can overcome a lot together."

Dan adds, "Prayer is one of the most powerful things someone can do. Ask God to renew their minds and to give them victory. I don't think showering them with information, etc., is going to help … One of the things I've noticed about people with an eating disorder is they are normally strong-willed … I don't believe you'll get anywhere by applying pressure. They and God are the only ones who can lick this problem."

And finally, says Grace, "Help them see the truth, and that you love them no matter what. Then, get them help and follow through."

Chapter 22

Andrew

Andrew's Story

Recognizing

Gaining Control

FOR 21-YEAR-OLD Andrew, anorexia nervosa stemmed from an identity crisis.

"I had a friend growing up and was always trying to be just like him," recalls Andrew. "Then I started lifting weights at age 16, and became Andrew the Body Builder. Later, at age 17, I became Andrew the Cyclist."

It was this cyclist identity that spun him downhill, fast. "I was very competitive and wanted to do whatever it took to get faster," says Andrew, the third of four home-schooled children. He became very aware of his body during this time.

"I would look down at my stomach and think about how big it looked to me." Having seen photos of other pro-cyclists, he desired to look like them.

"I would picture them in my mind, how thin they looked," he recalls. "I started to cut back on my food selection and train longer in order to burn more calories. I would body-check, too. Pinch my skin. See how far my fingers could reach around my arms and ankles. Weigh myself a couple of times a day."

In spite of these obsessive tendencies, Andrew didn't realize he had an eating disorder; rather, he just thought he was being a dedicated athlete. "I remember losing weight through cycling and not thinking there was anything wrong," he says. "I was a cyclist, which meant I had to be skinny."

But then his skin started to turn yellow around his armpits, feet, hands and mouth. "My parents became concerned," he states. "They had been concerned about the weight loss, but I always had what I thought was a good excuse for it."

It took four different doctors before someone took Andrew's situation seriously and said his habits could be the warning signs for anorexia. "I thought, *Okay, no big deal. I just have to eat*," recalls Andrew.

But eating proved harder than he'd thought. For two weeks he piled on the food. Then, "I started to see that I was gaining weight." He became uncomfortable with how he looked and began to restrict again.

Months later he visited with a dietitian, who became very concerned after discovering Andrew's views of both food and his body. "She told me if I didn't make some changes, I would end up in a treatment center. I didn't believe her for a minute."

Andrew didn't think he had a problem. He was a cyclist. "If I wasn't biking, I wouldn't care about being so thin."

A couple more months went by, and Andrew lost more weight. Having just turned 19, "I remember telling my mom, 'Maybe I do have a problem.' " It scared him, but he still didn't want to change.

Familial Response

"Mom and Dad did what they could as parents, but there was only so much they could do," Andrew says. He would make excuses for why he wasn't eating, and, with this being new to all of them, they believed him. "Nobody really knew what to do for me."

His parents asked how they could help, but Andrew didn't know how to respond. He simply told them, "I don't know. You're asking the wrong person.

"It's hard when you don't hear much about eating disorders," explains Andrew, "especially in males."

Reacting

Losing Control

In September of 2007, Andrew was training for the provincial road bike championship. He had lost a lot of weight, to the point where people were noticing. "I was abnormally skinny," he says.

A couple of days after the race, Andrew had trouble getting his heart rate to go up while training. "I didn't seem to have strength or energy." He was forced to turn his bike around and go home.

"Eventually, I had to quit training all together." He was choosing to lose weight, even at the expense of cycling. "I found this to be scary and upsetting."

When he tried to eat more, he somehow wasn't able to. "Anorexia had too much control over me," Andrew says. "I was no longer able to do what I wanted. The eating disorder was making my decisions for me."

Familial Response

"By now my family was very worried and scared," says Andrew. They'd started to look into treatment centers, feeling there was no other option. "Mom and Dad had done what they could, but now I needed more."

He was put on a waiting list for Homewood Health Center in Guelph, Ontario, and in December of 2007, they received the call. Andrew had been accepted.

"My parents had to take me, kicking and screaming," he says. "I cried the whole way down, staring out the window, thinking this had to be a dream."

Peak Point

Prior to graduating from Homewood in April of 2008, Andrew had already started to relapse.

After arriving home, "I started biking three hours a day and eating half-portions of food." The weight he'd put on at Homewood fell off, and in less than a month, he was worse than he'd been prior to the center.

"By now I was eating two salads a day. I didn't have energy for anything. Mostly I sat in my room all day doing puzzles, watching movies or writing." And at night, he couldn't sleep. "If I dozed off, it wouldn't be for long," Andrew recalls.

Spiritually Speaking

"I was living a hell on earth," Andrew says. Having accepted Christ long before developing anorexia, Andrew knew it was impossible to be separated from God; but he says, "The distance I felt from God was unbelievable."

Andrew had never felt so alone in his life. "It was the worst feeling I have ever felt. I was at rock bottom."

People everywhere were praying for Andrew. "Churches were praying for me. People who didn't know anything except that a young man had anorexia, were praying."

He knew he had to make a choice. The next step for anorexia was death. "I had to decide if that was what I really wanted. I had been struggling with the demon for so long and just wanted it to end. The only way I saw for my struggle to end was to give in to anorexia and die."

He now understands that this was Satan's plan for him, all along.

Recovery

Andrew recalled something his doctor had said. He'd told Andrew, "You have to make a choice whether you want to live or die. The time for choosing life is almost up."

"I chose life," said Andrew. "I wanted to give life another chance. Giving up was not an option."

That very night, he prayed to God, and then slept. He woke up the next morning before anyone else, and ate breakfast. It was the first time he'd eaten breakfast in months.

"I noticed soon after that, that I didn't have to fight like I did before. Satan didn't seem to have control anymore." He no longer heard the voice in his head, telling him what choices to make. And for the first time in a long time, he smiled. "It was a feeling like no other."

Andrew knew he had a long road ahead of him.

"I needed to start working right away on my weight restoration." So he told his mom that he was ready to recover. And, using the information he'd learned at Homewood, he set up a treatment plan for himself, filling out menus and eating extra portions. "I did most of my recovery on my own," he says.

His parents were unsure what to think. "They didn't want to do something that would make me change my mind [and so] they held back, and watched to see what would happen with me."

Andrew ended up seeing a counselor, weekly, someone with whom to talk about his recovery and progress. "He was able to give me some tips from his experience with helping other recovering anorexics."

Renewal

By spring of 2010, Andrew was doing construction and living on his own in London. One day, he received a call from his mom, asking to take him out to lunch to Swiss Chalet. "I was kind of excited," Andrew says.

While battling anorexia, eating out had proven a struggle. "I would research the menu beforehand," Andrew recalls, "and find the lowest calorie meals." Most of the time, he'd eat salads, picking out the extras and refusing to use dressing.

"During our lunch, Mom looked at my chicken wrap and plate of fries, and asked if this was still a struggle," Andrew says. "I looked up with a smile and said, 'Not at all. I'm not even thinking about the calories. All I'm thinking about is how good this tastes, and the fact that I can spend lunch with you.'"

He ended up eating his meal, and part of his mom's meal. "That was too much," he says with a laugh. "But it didn't bother me."

He is now training again and competing as a professional cyclist. "It's definitely been a process," says Andrew. "I really had to ease back into training slowly, and constantly check in with people around me to make sure I stayed healthy. It doesn't consume me any longer. Spending time with my family and friends has become most important to me now. They have always been my biggest fans and greatest support team. I couldn't be happier having them back in my life so close to me."

He now realizes the illness started when he put cycling before

God. "When I was ready to work towards having God first in my life again, there was a book I found that helped me, called Who I Am in Christ by Neil T. Anderson (Regal, 2001). It talked about God's love for me and what that means." He uses the truths found in that book to rebuke Satan and his lies on a daily basis.

Parents' Perspective

Recognizing

Louise and Harold recognized there was something wrong when Andrew was 15.

"He often got in the dumps," says Louise. "He believed he did not have a good life. He and I spoke many, many times about it. I tried to show him the truth about his situation and challenge his thinking. What none of us realized at the time, but seems obvious in hindsight, was that Andrew was struggling with depression."

Having started cycling at the age of 12, Andrew's hobby turned obsession when he began to ride competitively five years later. "He had to eat healthy and at certain times," says Louise. "There was a schedule for everything, and if the family didn't do it his way, then it was construed as a lack of support on our part."

At 18, a coach took interest in Andrew. "He gave dietary suggestions to maximize performance," recalls Harold. "Andrew took these very seriously and almost became obsessed by them."

Then, Andrew began overtraining. "He always had good reasons for what he did," says Louise, "and could justify why he needed to bike longer or leave something from his diet."

Sponsored by Champion Cycle, Andrew started competing at an expert level in the summer of 2006. Placing first in the standings for the province much of the season, "He had great talent, and it showed," says Harold.

Yet training had become more important than the actual race. Harold knew there was a problem when Andrew, who was scheduled to race in Elliot Lake, did not want to go because it would cut into his training time.

"That really bothered me," says Harold. "I couldn't make any sense of it, as all this training was for the racing. I felt huge disbelief. I couldn't understand how Andrew could lose his passion as an athlete, and replace it with a pattern of living that could eventually kill him."

Triggers and Signals

Looking back, Harold and Louise recognized the following triggers for their son's illness:

- Depression
- A desire to make something of himself
- A desire to be in control of his own life
- Louise's tendency to control, and Harold's perfectionist streak.

Signs that Andrew had anorexia:
- Fatigue
- Bowel problems
- Digestive problems
- Very rigid mealtimes
- Didn't allow himself carbohydrates
- Drank countless mugs of green tea
- Never ate in the evening
- Never let himself have treats
- Seemed unable to follow the dietitian's food plans
- Often trained beyond the time required
- Began to withdraw from family and friends
- Did not attend any function that would influence his training schedule

Reacting

As time went on, Andrew's malnourishment began to exhibit itself through health problems. In addition to gastro-intestinal difficulties, his skin turned yellow, suggesting a malfunctioning liver.

In spite of numerous trips to the doctor's office, they never saw the same doctor more than once. They said he was thin but never went beyond that. Finally, one of the medical professionals asked if Andrew had an eating disorder. Around the same time Andrew had started seeing a dietitian who confirmed that yes, Andrew was indeed anorexic. That was April of 2007.

"The news was disturbing but really held no meaning for me," says Louise. "The dietitian suggested we see a psychiatrist, but we didn't think we needed it at that point. We felt sure it was fixable and that with help, we would get things on track." The dietitian never told them that people could die from it.

It wasn't long before they were in over their heads. "We had no idea where to turn," says Louise. "We did not have a family doctor, and we needed help." Then, a new doctor came to town—an athlete—who met Andrew at the YMCA.

One Sunday, when Andrew was suffering severe abdominal pains, Louise and Harold took him to Emergency, praying that this particular doctor would be in. "He was there and was very friendly. He told Andrew he needed a doctor and offered to be his physician. What a blessing!" says Louise. "In the days to come, we would praise God many times for bringing this man into our family's life."

By the end of 2007, anorexia had become a full-scale addiction. Just before Christmas, Andrew was admitted to the Homewood Health Centre. "He would not/could not cooperate in the treatment center and was engaging in his behaviors even while he was there," says Louise. "By now the entire family was trying to watch how we spoke about food and weight. We even asked people who came to the house to be careful how they spoke and what they said. A no-food discussion policy was in effect." It didn't seem to make a difference, though.

Recovery

While it took much more than Homewood for Andrew to recover, Louise and Howard are both grateful to the program for saving Andrew's life.

"There were many things about [it] that we did not always appreciate, but at the time, it was our only option," says Harold. "It seemed the staff was always changing, and the program was constantly under revision. This meant lack of continuity, and sometimes cancelled programs that the patients needed."

As with many centers, the treatment model was conducted through group therapy. "Very little was done privately to see what was driving each one to do what they did," says Louise. "Still, God can use things that are less than perfect."

Harold and Louise made weekly visits to Homewood and called regularly. They attended each of the parent and family counseling days. Andrew fostered anger towards Harold and so spent hours communicating with Louise, either on the phone or in person. Harold wrote letters, and the family made a point of visiting and taking gifts.

While Andrew did not accept the program well, "he did get somewhat better, and was no longer in physical danger," says Louise.

Nevertheless, the spiritual and mental aspects of the illness were not addressed; as a result, Andrew continued to battle destructive thought patterns upon arriving home in April 2008.

Three weeks to live

In spite of familial support and Christian counseling, Andrew's battle with food ensued. By the end of summer 2008, he was critically ill again. "Our doctor met with us and told us that if Andrew did not choose to live, he could not survive more than another three weeks," recalls Harold.

The doctor had one final suggestion: in-home visits by a psychiatric nurse. She came twice a week. "That was the first glimmer of hope," says Louise. "She was very good with Andrew---completely non-judgmental."

Around this time, Andrew showed some interest in getting a kitten. "We got him one, and he enjoyed that. He started to come out of himself."

Three weeks later, he decided that maybe he could get better. "That was the beginning of a road to recovery," says Louise. "By that fall, Andrew was well enough to start work. Later, he moved to London."

Spiritually Speaking

"There was anger, but it was not at God," says Louise. She doesn't believe it was God's desire for Andrew to become anorexic.

"However, He allowed it as a logical consequence of destructive personal habits and thought processes."

Meeting with a Christian counselor helped them to face their perfectionist and controlling behaviors. "We did a lot of spiritual housecleaning," says Harold. "It was an amazing experience. It helped us to be much more united than we were prior."

While their marriage had always been strong, "counseling brought us much closer and gave us a bond we would need in the days to come," says Louise. "God used it to prepare us for the difficult days ahead."

Choice Morsels

For parents or spouses with eating-disordered loved ones, Louise and Harold offer the following tips:

• Be aware of your God-given instincts. If you think there is a problem, you are probably right.
• Take this illness seriously; it is not a passing phase that will just go away.
• Recognize that body checking, excessive exercise, and obsession with weight are not normal.
• Share with others in the family of God, and with those who love you. Send letters and updates to families and friends so they might pray.
• Ask your church to send cards and other gestures of encouragement to your loved one.
• Do your homework when it comes to treatment centers. There are many options, but few that deal with the spiritual aspect of the illness; even fewer that handle males.
• Don't neglect the rest of your family; they see what is going on and they need to process this, too.
• Spend time with the Lord. *Streams in the Desert* by L.B. Cowman (Zondervan, 1999) is an excellent devotional for times of trial.
• Put on the armor of God each day and fight for your loved one.

- Keep trusting the Lord.
- Don't give up. Recovery is a long process. The illness didn't come in a day, and, barring a miracle, will not be gone in a day either. Give it time.

Chapter 23

Mary

Mary's Story

FOR MARY, A FAMILY PHYSICIAN and mother of three, anorexia nervosa is more than a term in a medical text. Having nearly died from it in high school, Mary knows the intricacies of the sickness from a very personal perspective.

Recognizing

Excelling at school, dominating in sports, and coming from a supportive and loving family, "Many looking at my life would have thought I 'had it all,' " says Mary. Yet, having a Type-A perfectionist personality, she constantly expected more of herself. "I was my own worst enemy."

Like many of her friends, Mary wished to be thinner and prettier. Despite being popular amongst females and males, she never felt attractive. Meanwhile, "I competed at a local and national level in track and field, and won many competitions."

The summer she turned 16, Mary decided she wanted more. She thought perhaps if she worked harder, she could become an Olympian, and so, spent hours each day training. "This was the beginning of my rapid spiral downwards into anorexia."

Reacting

One thing led to another. Mary thought by eating healthier, she'd perform better. Eating healthier soon became "eating less."

She began to restrict calories and to obsess over food. By this point she was training upwards of six hours a day, and eating next to nothing.

"But, as other anorexics know, nothing you achieve is ever good enough," Mary says. The more she trained and the less she ate, the weaker she became until she was too weak to compete.

"Within a matter of four months I had dropped over 40 pounds." Entering grade 12 that fall, Mary was a faint image of herself. She spiraled into dark depression and could barely function.

"My mother quickly recognized what was happening and confronted me," says Mary. "She had also battled an eating disorder during university, and although she had fought to protect her own children from the same fate, the evil one had other plans."

In December of that year, Mary was admitted to SickKids. After spending more than seven weeks in treatment, "I was discharged home physically stronger, but mentally very ill."

The next two years were filled with trips to various treatment facilities as Mary battled depression and malnutrition. "I came close to death's doorstep many times, and even attempted to kill myself by swallowing a bottle of Extra Strength Tylenol," she recalls. "I felt so helpless—like I was possessed by evil."

She remembers a relentless string of negative thoughts churning through her mind. She couldn't sleep at night for their presence.

Recovery

Eventually, Mary voluntarily entered Homewood Health Center, where she spent five months trying to recover. "Unfortunately, ignoring the spiritual side of this illness is a grave mistake many people and treatment programs make," she says. "I was so angry at God for 'allowing' me to go through this that I shut Him out of my life."

Mary's parents continued to pray, however, as did family and friends. "They were my warriors when I couldn't be," Mary says.

There was no major turning point, yet as Mary returned home and re-entered high school, "small things started to change." Each meal was still a battle, she recalls, but this time she decided to fight.

As a result, "I noticed that things got a little bit easier." The more she nourished her body, the clearer her thoughts became. "I finally started to recognize the lies of anorexia, and the subtle ways they could invade my life."

While her relationship with food was still far from normal, Mary was able to recognize that food provided the fuel she needed to function each day. "God gave me the will to want to live again, not just go through the motions."

As she started to forgive herself and to let go of the anger she'd fostered towards God, "real healing" began.

Renewal

Today Mary is a wife to an accountant, a mother to two boys and a girl, and a doctor in family medicine. While she doesn't pretend that the last 15 years have been free of struggle, she says, "God has granted me the awareness to recognize my temptations and weaknesses, and has surrounded me with people who have helped me through these difficult times. He keeps me accountable for my actions and decisions, and helps me to recognize the subtle lies and unhealthy habits so they won't drag me into further lies."

Healing Steps

Say a Little Prayer

Every day when Mary rises, she utters a prayer—a few simple words to God—asking Him to clothe her in heavenly armor, and to take control of her day. "This means I am making a conscious choice to live in His truth," she says. "It protects me from the lies of Satan, and the many devious ways he continually tries to destroy my sense of self."

After years of performing this exercise, "it becomes almost subconscious. It's so automatic and powerful that the lies of the evil one are that much easier to fight and ignore."

Walk in Truth

Following her daily prayer, Mary makes a conscious effort to walk in Truth. This translates into keeping her steps holy—swerving from temptation, and striving for righteous thoughts. "Knowing the depths from which I've come often serves as motivation enough to keep me from slipping into bad habits," she says. "My health directly affects the people around me. I want to be the kind of wife, mother, friend, daughter and sibling who is able to give and love completely."

When she allows Satan's lies to take her mind captive, she notices a shift in her priorities. "I stop looking after myself and the people I love." Through prayer, Mary now has the wisdom to recognize bad habits and falsehoods early on, "so they don't have the opportunity to take root in my life."

Choice Morsels

Come Clean
When it comes to parenting as a former anorexic, Mary advises living in redemption, and letting go of shame and guilt. "Some people try to hide their past struggles, and I can't stress enough how unhealthy this can be."

Children, in particular, are very intuitive, she says. "Early on, they will become aware of the fact that 'Mommy is hiding something,' and this creates an unhealthy environment of secrecy and uncertainty."

Instead, impress upon your children the importance of living in truth and light, by being an example to them. "Teach them to love themselves and to see their bodies through God's eyes."

With a picky eater for a son, Mary has learned to commit mealtimes to God. "As we have more children, I will continue to surround them with prayer and to talk to them openly and honestly about 'Mommy's past struggles.' "

She's also committed to refraining from making comments about her children's changing bodies, and to teaching them to love themselves regardless of their imperfections.

Know Yourself
If you've battled an eating disorder, you know there are triggers. "Just as a former addict needs to avoid situations that tempt them to resume unhealthy behaviors, anorexics need to do the same," says Mary.

Upon entering medical school, Mary thought her "calling" was to work with victims of anorexia and their families. But then she realized, "God had other plans for me." Doing that type of work, in fact, became an unhealthy trigger, causing her to return to some bad habits.

"The more the evil one loses his grip on you, the harder he will work to tempt you," she says. "He will try and sink his ugly teeth into you in any way he can—especially when he knows God is winning."

Recognize the situations that allow these temptations to take root. Then, choose to avoid these temptations, "sometimes many times a day." This, says Mary, is essential to winning the battle. "Don't fall victim to the belief that you are out of the woods, otherwise the 'thorn in your side' will return with a renewed vengeance."

In Christ Alone

"When the battle seems relentless, and you don't know how you're going to continue—that's when you must dig your heels in and trust," says Mary.

"The victory is in sight if you cling to God and to His promises. Choose to continue fighting, but don't think for a second that you're capable of doing it on your own. Only God can give you the strength and persistence required to make it through."

She recalls days in which she had to make the choice to continue fighting on a second-to-second basis. "And when you can't fight any longer, pray!" Mary urges. "Surround yourself with a cloud of witnesses who will also pray." If it weren't for the warriors in her life, she says, she wouldn't be here today.

Mary believes in continuous victory. Yet she also believes that (with a few exceptions), "like any other addiction, anorexia is something you will battle for the rest of your life."

As a result, former anorexics must choose, each day, to overcome temptation. "Don't let shame, arrogance or a sense of naivety make you feel invincible." Instead, know that God has granted you victory, and will continue to strengthen you in your walk as you seek His will and His way.

Chapter 24

Maureen

Maureen's Story

RETIRED PHYS ED TEACHER Maureen was able to sympathize with the struggles faced by her daughter, Mary, having gone through them herself when she was in university.

"It was a fairly typical scenario," the 60-year-old recalls. "I was a top student, very athletic (played varsity basketball and track), and had a healthy social network of friends. There seemed to be lots going for me. Some even thought I might compete at the Olympic level someday."

At the time, anorexia nervosa was largely un-researched and rarely spoken of, and so proved a lonely journey for the star athlete and scholar. "I was very much alone and helpless in the whole experience. I was unable to confide in others about my private hell."

Maureen felt trapped by constant thoughts of food and body image. Over a period of three years, she lost 45 pounds, exercised obsessively, developed some OCD tendencies and suffered from depression.

Recognizing

"Looking back, I see that figuring out my identity and accepting who I was, was very central to the disease," she says. Having grown up on a farm surrounded by a tight-knit family, leaving for university proved traumatic.

Around the same time, Maureen realized her goal of becoming an Olympic-level athlete was out of reach. "Food happened to be the one area that I latched on to and felt I could control."

She marvels that she emerged from those years alive. "I was not a Christian (although I knew Christian teachings) until several years later. Now, I can look back and see how God was taking care of me, even though I wasn't paying much attention to Him."

Reacting

Even at her worst, Maureen never once confided in anyone. "[My friends and family] would try to reason with me about it (they could see the physical and emotional toll it was taking on me), but I refused to acknowledge the problem outwardly."

She studied obsessively and continued to pursue athletics, despite performance levels deteriorating due to her weakness. "For me it truly was a 'secret' disease and I suffered in silence."

Recovery

For Maureen, healing was a long, arduous process. Being a perfectionist (having graduated from Queen's with highest standing in her class and being a provincial record holder in track and field and top scorer in varsity basketball), "university years were extremely stressful because being 'successful' was measured (mistakenly) by achievement."

When she graduated and started teaching, life became more bearable. "Some of the obsessive food and image thoughts gradually subsided." Marriage brought more balance to her life, yet she still struggled to talk about her "secret," even with her husband.

It wasn't until becoming pregnant that Maureen's body image truly began to heal. "Children helped to get my focus off me and onto the babies and, out of necessity in looking after four toddlers, thoughts of food and body image receded into the background," she says. "There were other more pressing priorities."

Upon becoming a believer in 1990, she says, "God completed my healing." While He did this in several ways, one that stands out occurred at a weekend retreat.

"The message was based on Psalm 139. It was as if God reached out and touched me with His truth. According to the Word, He knew all my thoughts—I didn't need to hide anything from Him because He already knows. 'I am fearfully and wonderfully made.' God made me just the way He wanted, complete with talents and flaws, and His works are wonderful. How could I question or dislike what He had made?"

As she read His Word that weekend, Maureen felt God embrace

191 | Chasing Silhouettes

her. He loved her the way she was. There was no need to worry about 'achieving'; no need to try to be perfect in the eyes of others.

"God 'knit me together' and created me the way He intended," she says. "That day, as I gazed over a peaceful lake with His beautiful creation all around me, God gave me the miracle of His love and healing and brought peace to my mind and body and soul as never before experienced."

Renewal

Thirty-five years later, Maureen continues to walk in her renewed identity. "I have no more thoughts of food or body image that hold me captive," she says. "My OCD habits have disappeared. Being successful in life is not measured by achievements but by my journey with the Lord and serving Him."

Eating disorders are multi-faceted diseases that require physical, emotional, mental, and spiritual healing. "The last one is a big one," says Maureen. "Many people have trouble recognizing or accepting the power of the enemy and the need to call upon the Lord for help. You can't do it alone."

Healing Steps

Quiet Time

One of the main ingredients in renewal, Maureen believes, consists of a deep relationship with the Creator.

"Having a 'quiet time' with God to pray and read Scripture each day is important," she says. "It's like guarding against evil by building my relationship with God. For me, this is first thing in the morning. If my day has an early start, then I get up earlier so that there is (nearly always) time for quiet time."

Pure Thoughts

Maureen holds fast to the message found in Matthew 12:43-45: "When an evil spirit comes out of a man, it goes through arid places seeking rest and does not find it. Then it says, 'I will return to the house I left.' When it arrives, it finds the house unoccupied, swept clean and put in order. Then it goes and takes with it seven other spirits more wicked than itself, and they go in and live there. And the final condition of that man is worse than the first."

In light of this verse, it's important to "occupy" your mind with thoughts of God, Maureen says; don't leave it empty for Satan to fill.

Rather, "Whatever is true, whatever is noble, whatever is right, whatever is pure, whatever is lovely, whatever is admirable—if anything is excellent or praiseworthy—think about such things." (Philippians 4:8) Then, God's love will be allowed to grow within you.

"When I have negative thoughts about myself, I remember Psalm 139, about how God created me to be perfect and wonderfully made in His eyes. What right do I have to find fault with God's creation?"

Body Guard

Quoting and memorizing Scripture, Maureen adds, helps to chase away the enemy. "Sometimes I keep verses of scripture in my pocket, which I can then pull out and read."

She urges putting on the armor of God daily (Ephesians 6: 10-18), and discerning, with God's guidance, any bonds of the enemy that may be preventing you from healing, breaking them in Jesus' name.

"Be on the alert from the enemy, and flee from him!" Maureen says. Keep from temptations such as food labels, weighing, pouring over recipes, looking at the mirror excessively, etcetera.

And finally, "Sing!" says Maureen, who praises God through song whenever she's alone. This will not only lift your spirit, but will keep the enemy at bay.

Kid Talk

In spite of trying fervently to teach her four children that God wanted them to care for their bodies, two of Maureen's daughters also battled acute anorexia.

"We tried to help our children live healthy lifestyles—good nutrition, adequate rest, healthy relationships, no smoking or drugs, lots of exercise, balance in their lives," says Maureen. "My husband and

I tried to model this lifestyle and consciously promote it. I tried to stay away from any focus on body image or fat content in food in fear that they would develop eating disorders … all to no avail."

Yet, having gone through anorexia herself, Maureen was able to sympathize with, and comprehend, the complexities of her daughters' battles, and to walk alongside them into the light of recovery. Today, both of her daughters (who share Maureen's driven, perfectionist personality) are living in renewal.

"Pray for your children," she urges. "Love them unconditionally. Help them see they are beautiful and perfect in God's eyes without changing their image. [And] try not to make food an issue [by urging them to finish what's on their plate, or forcing them to eat something they really don't like]."

In addition, she says, do not focus on body image, labels, or fashion magazines, and minimize your interest in clothes, makeup and accessories.

"Help your children understand that success in life is measured in many ways," says Maureen. "God wants them to do the best they can with the talents He gives them, but He also wants them to use those talents to benefit the work of His kingdom. The focus is to be God-centered, not me-centered."

Finally, "Walk as Jesus walked," says Maureen. "Reflect His love. Teach your children God's ways. Help them see that God made each of them uniquely, and He loves each of His creations (flaws and all!). Help them recognize and develop their talents and gifts and to use them well for God in their every-day life."

ACKNOWLEDGEMENTS

THERE ARE SO MANY names that bear mentioning, so many people who have believed in this project from Day One, so many voices that have added to the chorus, not the least of which is my agent, Sandra Bishop of MacGregor Literary, who never gave up. Despite numerous rejections for this niche project, she knew the need and kept believing. Even after I'd stopped.

Abundant thanks to my publisher, Jason Chatraw at Ampelon, for so fully and humbly coming alongside this project, and for Jennifer Wolf, who put hours into editing and guiding it.

To Dr. Gregory Jantz, for his commitment to helping *Chasing Silhouettes* succeed.

To Constance Rhodes, Founder of FINDINGbalance, for her advice, support and marketing skills.

To Ann Capper, Nutrition Advisor and Editor at FINDINGbalance, for wise and careful editing.

To Robert Irvin at Standard Publishing for helping the book become what it needed to be.

To Erin Baan, for selfless abandonment.

To Amy Huzil of Inspired Creativity for her generosity and inspiration.

To Dr. Carylynn Larson of Rock Recovery for consistently applauding the project.

To Ron Broughton, Dr. Amy Wasserbauer, Dr. Dena Cabrera, Len Thompson, Bernard Hubbard and Rachel Koprowski for the time and energy they poured into interviews and endorsements.

To Helen and Danica Burns; to Harold, Louise and Andrew House; to Dan Wagner, Karen (Grace) Amos and Constance Rhodes; and to Maureen Lisle and Mary Nyvall for so humbly and transparently sharing their stories.

To Melissa Bob, Marney Stewart, Sarah Bingham and Jennifer Zidek for being my friends through it all.

And to my family: to Keith, Allison and Meredith—for forgiving me, and for being willing to help other siblings find hope and healing on this hard journey; to my parents, Ernest and Yvonne Dow—for never stopping believing in me. Even when I screamed in your faces. I am who I am because of you.

To my husband, Trenton Nathan, for showing me the face of Christ. For teaching me freedom and grace, and what it means to love. To my boys, Aiden Grey and Kasher Jude—you are my life.

And above all, to my Lord and Savior Jesus Christ, for whom and to whom I am forever indebted.

Thank you.
e.

RECOMMENDED RESOURCES

Alcorn, N. 2008. *Beyond Starved: Real Stories, Real Freedom.* WinePress Publishing.

Alcorn, N. 2007. *Starved: Mercy for Eating Disorders.* Wine-Press Publishing.

Brumberg, J. 2000. *Fasting Girls: The History of Anorexia Nervosa.* Vintage. New York, NY.

Collins, L. 2004. *Eating With Your Anorexic: How My Child Recovered Through Family Based Treatment and Yours Can Too.* Mc-Graw-Hill Companies, Inc. New York, NY.

Heaton, J. and C. Strauss. 2005. *Talking to Eating Disorders: Simple Ways to Support Someone Who Has Anorexia, Bulimia, Binge Eating, or Body Image Issues.* New American Library Publishing (Penguin Group). New York, NY.

Hornbacher, M. 1998. *Wasted: A Memoir of Anorexia and Bulimia.* HarperCollins Publishers. New York, NY.

Lucas, A. 2004. *Demystifying Anorexia Nervosa: An Optimistic Guide to Understanding and Healing.* Oxford University Press. New York, NY.

Orr, T. 2007. *When the Mirror Lies – Anorexia, Bulimia, and Other Eating Disorders.* Franklin Watts Publishing (Scholastic Inc.). New York, NY.

Pettit, C. 2006. *Empty – A Story of Anorexia.* Fleming H. Revell Publishing (Baker Publishing Group). Grand Rapids, MI.

Pipher, M. 1994. *Reviving Ophelia.* Ballantine. New York, NY.

Rhodes, C. 2003. *Life Inside the "Thin" Cage.* Shaw Books.

Samelson, D. 2009. *Feeding the Starving Mind: A Personalized, Comprehensive Approach to Overcoming Anorexia and Other Starvation Eating Disorders.* New Harbinger Publications, Inc. Oakland, CA.

ABOUT THE AUTHOR

EMILY WIERENGA is the author of two books, an award-winning freelance journalist, a commissioned artist, wife and mother. She battled anorexia nervosa both as a child and as an adult, and has appeared as a guest multiple times on Canada's premiere Christian television talk show and radio talk-back program. Emily also serves as an Official Ambassador for FINDINGbalance, and as a Navigator for the National Eating Disorder Association, and is a popular speaker at retreats, conferences, churches and schools.

To connect with Emily, vist her website at: **EmilyWierenga.com**

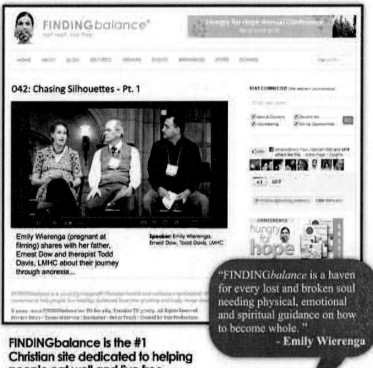